1981

REPRESENTATIVE AMERICAN SPEECHES 1979-1980

edited by **WALDO W. BRADEN**
Boyd Professor of Speech
Louisiana State University

THE REFERENCE SHELF

Volume 52 Number 5

THE H. W. WILSON COMPANY

New York   1980

THE REFERENCE SHELF

The books in this series contain reprints of articles, excerpts from books, and addresses on current issues and social trends in the United States and other countries. There are six separately bound numbers in each volume, all of which are generally published in the same calendar year. One number is a collection of recent speeches; each of the others is devoted to a single subject and gives background information and discussion from various points of view, concluding with a comprehensive bibliography. Books in the series may be purchased individually or on subscription.

Library of Congress Catalog Card

Representative American speeches, 1937/38–
  New York, H. W. Wilson Co.
               v.21.cm.annual. (The Reference shelf)
    Editors: 1937/38–1958/59, A. C. Baird.–1959/60–1969/70,
        L. Thonssen.–1970/71–1979/80, W. W. Braden.
  I. American orations.   2. Speeches, addresses, etc.
I. Baird, Albert Craig, ed.   II. Thonssen, Lester,
ed.   III. Braden, Waldo W., ed.   IV. Series.
PS668.B3   815.5082   38–27962

International Standard Book Number 0-8242-0648-7
PRINTED IN THE UNITED STATES OF AMERICA

CONTENTS

SCIENCE AND TECHNOLOGY

CELEBRATION OF SPECIAL TIMES

CONSCIENCE AND COMMITMENT

PREFACE

OVERVIEW OF PUBLIC ADDRESS IN THE SEVENTIES

Theodore C. Sorenson, adviser and speech writer for John F. Kennedy, recently wrote that "relatively few public addresses of our time will be included in future editions of 'The World's Greatest Orations'" (*NY Times Magazine*, Ag. 19, '79, p 7). This statement certainly applies to the 190 speeches that have appeared in *Representative American Speeches* since 1970. In particular, presidential speech has been pedestrian. Richard M. Nixon, erratic and insincere, seemed aggressive and stereotyped in his utterances. Gerald Ford, making no claim as a speaker, was earnest, but flat and bland. Jimmy Carter, striving for informality, was low keyed, folksy, and sometimes halting.

Likewise, speeches given by members of the Senate and House of Representatives attracted little attention. Certainly, no politician of the decade could match the wit, charm, and rapport that Adlai Stevenson demonstrated in his two tries for the presidency in the nineteen fifties. All in all, the presidential primaries, the national political conventions, and the final campaigns for the presidency in 1972 and 1976 were little more than media events or as one writer said recently "prolonged media circuses." The 1980 campaign promised to be no better than the others. Dropping by the wayside among the Republicans have been John Connally (Texas), Howard Baker (Tennessee), Phillip M. Crane (Illinois), and Robert Dole (Kansas). After the Wisconsin primary in April, Edmund Brown Jr. of California withdrew from the Democratic primaries. By late April the races narrowed to contests between Ronald Reagan (California) and George Bush (Texas) on the Republican side and between incumbent Jimmy Carter and Edward Kennedy (Massachusetts) on the Democratic side.

During the primaries, the Republicans staged some good

5

television shows, including some so-called debates among the contenders in Iowa, New Hampshire, South Carolina, and Texas. On the other hand, Senator Kennedy was unable to draw President Carter, who was busy with international and home crises, out of the "Rose Garden" in Washington until after May 1. Kennedy complained bitterly about not having opportunities earlier to face the President at the hustings. John Anderson, liberal Republican Representative from Illinois, announced on April 24 that instead of continuing to seek the Republican nomination, he would run as an Independent.

During the seventies the best public address was non-political. Judged by what has been included in *Representative American Speeches*, these speeches occurred on those occasions when the audience or the occasion made special demands upon the speaker: bicentennial celebrations; college and university convocations, lectureships, and institutes; meetings of private foundations and business groups; judicial conferences; special interest group meetings, particularly among blacks and women; and international meetings. Meetings of this sort required the speakers to prepare very carefully and often resulted in wide circulation of speeches through broadcasts and printed versions.

Some speakers of the decade, of course, stand out above the others. Among the better academic speakers have been Theodore M. Hesburgh of the University of Notre Dame and William J. McGill of Columbia University. In the Senate, Frank Church (Democrat) of Idaho, Edmund Muskie (Democrat) of Maine, Mark O. Hatfield (Republican) of Oregon, and Charles McC. Mathias (Republican) of Maryland have excelled. Vernon Jordan Jr., President of the National Urban League, has given some very significant speeches.

Some speeches are memorable: Daniel Moynihan before the United Nations (1977); Barbara Jordan before the National Democratic Convention in 1976; Sol M. Linowitz, upon receiving the Charles E. Wilson Award in 1977 ("Let the Candles Be Brought") and Francis B. Sayre Jr.'s "Tall Ships," Bicentennial Sermon (June 27, 1976) at Trinity Church at Newport, Rhode Island.

Other occasions (all covered in *Representative American Speeches* volumes) that brought forth significant public address were the televised hearings of the House Committee on the Judiciary that considered the impeachment of President Richard M. Nixon in 1974; the Bicentennial Commemoration in 1976; Hubert Humphrey's return to the Senate in 1977 and his subsequent death; the announcement of the Camp David Accords between Egypt and Israel from the White House in 1978; and the visit of Pope John Paul II to the United States in 1979.

In assembling the present volume the editor has received many kindnesses and much needed help from speakers, their assistants, and program chairmen. As always, his colleagues at Louisiana State University have been most supportive. David Cornell, President of Westminster College, in Salt Lake City, Utah, has supplied copies of many speeches. The editors at the H. W. Wilson Company have been most discerning. The support of John H. Pennybacker, chairman of the Department of Speech of Louisiana State University, has eased the tasks of editing the speeches. The manuscript could never have been finished without secretarial help of Jean Jackson, Stephanie Ducote, and especially Myra Fitts.

Waldo W. Braden[1]

August 1980
Baton Rouge, Louisiana

---

[1] For biographical note, see Appendix.

AMERICAN FOREIGN POLICY

A REVIEW OF THE FOREIGN POLICY[1]

HENRY A. KISSINGER [2]

On April 10, 1980 at 2:30 P.M., Henry A. Kissinger, former Secretary of State, addressed the annual convention of the American Society of Newspaper Editors, meeting in the Center Ballroom of the Washington Hilton Hotel. He spoke immediately following an hour-long speech and question-and-answer session by President Jimmy Carter. In the course of the meeting, the editors also heard Ronald Reagan, Edward Kennedy, and John Anderson speak.

In his book the *White House Years* (1979), Kissinger had stated his position on US foreign policy: "For as far ahead as we can see America's task will be to recreate and maintain the two pillars of our policy . . . a willingness to confront Soviet expansion and a simultaneous readiness to mark out a cooperative future." Developing this theme in the present speech, he delivered a sharp attack on the shortcomings of the Carter Administration's foreign policy, in particular its "profound ambivalence about the role of power in the world." As a world diplomat, and adviser to President Nixon, former Secretary of State, and widely published author on foreign affairs, Kissinger enjoys great prestige and his views command respect both here and abroad.

James Reston of the New York *Times* (April 11, 1980) offered his usual perceptive criticism of the speakers. Ronald Reagan, Reston wrote, "gave the editors the same old chicken-circuit Republican fund-raising arguments—hurrying breathlessly through his text. Nobody applauded until the end." The President "got respectful applause." Senator Kennedy "stuck to his basic campaign speech," and John Anderson spoke "without making any new impressions on the editors." Reston reserved his praise for Kissinger saying that he "made the only really Presidential speech . . . and with his sweep of history, made all the others seem almost trivial." William F. Buckley Jr. also thought Kissinger's speech was "the best speech delivered over the past season" (Baton Rouge *Morning Advocate*, Ap. 17, '80).

---

[1] Delivered at the annual convention of the American Society of Newspaper Editors, Center Ballroom, Washington Hilton Hotel, Washington, D.C., 2:30 P.M. April 19, 1980. Title supplied by editor. Quoted by permission.
[2] For biographical note, see Appendix.

This sobering speech on American foreign policy is clearly thought out, well organized, and so exceptionally well-articulated that there can be no doubt about Kissinger's meaning. It should be noted that the optimism expressed at the end tends to soften the impact of the cold, hard facts and observations presented throughout.

We are at the beginning of another of our quadrennial debates over foreign policy. Its forms have become as stylized as a Japanese kabuki play. The party in office claims that it inherited a debacle and by a near-miraculous effort has raised our prestige to new heights. The party out of office assails the current debacle and promises a radically new start.

This process courts two dangers. For our own public, it creates the impression that the foreign policy of the United States reflects only the idiosyncrasies of whoever is the incumbent. It masks a fundamental lesson which we seem to have forgotten: that the national interest of the United States does not change in years divisible by four.

And for the other nations of the world, the controversy is profoundly unsettling, whether they are foes watching in bewilderment or friends observing in dismay. America is the linchpin of the free world's security, the repository of the world's hope for progress. If every four years the basic premises of our foreign policy are up for grabs, America itself becomes an element of instability in the world. We give our friends an incentive to free themselves of the vagaries of our political process; we sow the psychological seeds of neutralism.

Therefore, our national debate must take place in a framework that permits us to work together as a united people after the election is over.

I supported the administration on the ratification of the Panama Canal treaties, Middle East arms sales, the Camp David agreement, the retaliatory steps in response to Afghanistan; and I worked to find a nonpartisan basis for SALT. No doubt I did not always ascribe to my successors the clear vision and profound wisdom that in hindsight I associate with my stewardship. Other Republicans, too, may well have strayed from the calm, disinterested analysis which all of us normally associate with the Grand Old Party.

But a major responsibility for setting the tone of our national debate rests with the incumbents. And the present administration, frankly, has been unusually partisan. An administration that can claim that it "rejuvenated" a "weak and dispirited" NATO Alliance, that it is the first to have friendly relations with both Japan and China, raises doubts about its grasp of reality. An administration capable of the innuendo that President Ford, one of the most decent men ever to occupy the Presidency, needlessly risked American lives for a transient popularity in a previous hostage situation tempts an equally unworthy examination of its own motives in the present situation. An administration that in its fourth year in office continues to blame its predecessors for every difficulty, and indeed seems to have made the confession of prior error a key instrument of policy, invites the question whether anyone relying on us does not run the risk of later disavowal. One cannot make history by rewriting it. A government's job is to find solutions to its problems, not alibis.

Whoever is victorious in November will find that he needs a unified people behind him because he will face a monumental challenge in foreign affairs. I happen to agree with President Carter that the danger to our country is the gravest in the modern period. We are sliding towards a world out of control, with our relative military power declining, with our economic lifeline increasingly vulnerable to blackmail, with hostile radical forces growing in every continent, and with the number of countries willing to stake their future on our friendship dwindling.

We did not arrive at this point áll at once or during one administration—though I believe that this administration has accelerated the most dangerous trends. Our peril is structural and conceptual. It requires a sustained national effort over an extended period of time whoever shall be the next President—or the next and the next as well. There are, I believe, four interrelated issues that must be addressed: First, the military balance; second, the geopolitical equation; third, the attitude towards the process of change in the world; and fourth, US-Soviet relations.

The Balance of Military Power

First of all, it can no longer be seriously denied that the overall military balance is shifting sharply against us. Every objective observer—such as the International Institute of Strategic Studies in London—has reached this grim conclusion. Whatever the causes, unless current trends are reversed, the 1980s will be a period of vulnerability such as we have not experienced since the early days of the Republic. In this decade we confront, for the first time, a potentially unfavorable strategic balance; a shifting balance against us in theater nuclear forces in Europe; and continuation of the long-standing Western inferiority in forces for regional defense.

Perhaps we are fortunate that the Iranian and Afghanistan crises illuminated our military deficiencies while the full extent of the danger was still in the future. Once awakened, we have the opportunity to redress the balance. If they do nothing else, these events *must* remind us of our inability to project forces quickly into vital regions, or else they will be the precursor of even graver challenges.

For thirty years the defense of the free world relied on our strategic superiority to compensate for our inferiority in conventional forces. That period has now ended—perhaps inevitably. Once we lost the ability to destroy the Soviet retaliatory forces at acceptable cost to ourselves, a general nuclear war spelled mutual suicide. Last year in Brussels I pointed out that a strategy relying on such a threat is incredible; irresponsible, and escapist—even for NATO. I was severely criticized—today's equivalent of shooting the messenger to avoid the message. But a danger ignored is a debacle invited. A country that can defend its interests only by threatening the mutual mass extermination of civilians dooms itself to strategic, and therefore eventually geopolitical, paralysis.

Rarely in history has a nation so passively accepted such a radical change in the military balance. Never in history has an opponent achieved as large an advantage in so many significant categories of military power without attempting to translate it into some political benefit.

The danger is less an imminent nuclear attack on us, than an increased Soviet willingness to run risks in local conflicts. And that seems to me the minimum consequence of what is ahead. We live in a world in turmoil; the safest prediction is continuing instability, some of it promoted by the Soviet Union, some of it only exploited by it. Since 1975, in Africa, in the Middle East, in Southeast Asia, radical forces with Soviet weapons, or Cuban proxy troops, and now the Red Army itself, have determined the outcome in almost every local conflict, to the detriment of our allies and friends. If this process continues and leads to direct US-Soviet confrontations, like that in Cuba in 1962 or the Mideast alert in 1973, it will be the *Soviet Union* which will possess the quantitative superiority in strategic weapons that *we* enjoyed when those and comparable crises were successfully resolved in our favor. And the Soviet local advantage has grown exponentially. Thus regional conflicts, whether deliberately promoted or not, threaten increasingly to exceed our ability to respond unless we drastically reverse the growing imbalance in *all* categories of military power.

We will pay a heavy penalty if we continue to take comfort in soporific assurances that our military establishment is still "second to none." It is this complacency which has brought us to our present pass over an extended period of time. In the 1960s, American strategic doctrine based deterrence largely on our theoretical capacity to inflict civilian casualties and economic damage on the Soviet Union, regardless of the size of the Soviet forces. This confused strategy with economic analysis. It not only overlooked the moral inhibitions that would surely affect an American President's willingness to launch such an attack; it also encouraged equanimity in the face of the relentless Soviet strategic buildup. Then in the early 1970s, a Vietnam-era anti-military sentiment assaulted *every* defense program whether or not it related to Vietnam. The anti-ballistic missile system (the ABM) passed the Senate by just one vote in 1969; forty Senators then tried to stop all our MIRV testing; in 1971 we barely defeated the Mansfield amendment to cut our forces in Europe by 150,000 men; in 1973 the Trident submarine program passed the Senate by only one vote. It was not until the advent of President Ford that these trends were reversed.

Fairness requires the recognition that President Carter thus inherited a difficult situation. But it must also be noted that the present administration has compounded the problem by systematically deprecating the role of power, by cancelling or stretching out every strategic program it inherited, by treating the whole defense budget more as a bargaining chip to win approval for SALT than as a serious instrument of national policy. History judges leaders by the adequacy of their response, not the magnitude of the challenge.

To be sure, in the current defense budget there are increases, somewhere between three and five percent. But the baseline for these calculations is unclear; the inflation rate is underestimated or hedged; key costs are understated. It turns out that the *real* increase is closer to one percent—or nearly irrelevant to the magnitude of the problem we face. And in any event, the adequacy of our response is not measured in the percentage of budgetary increase but by whether we are closing the gaps which every objective study reveals. And these gaps are simply not being closed; in fact many of them are still growing.

For a few weeks after the Soviet invasion of Afghanistan, it seemed that we had learned some lessons. And I therefore made several speeches in Europe urging hesitant allies to support the administration. Since then we are sliding back to our posture of ambivalence. Despite the invasion of Afghanistan, the President submitted precisely the defense budget that had been prepared *before* Afghanistan and on the expectation that SALT would be ratified. How can that possibly be adequate when in the meantime we have undertaken a major new defense commitment embracing the Persian Gulf? Since then even that budget appears to have been cut further in the new anti-inflation program. Nor do the projected forces show any sense of urgency. The MX missile is planned for 1987.

The air- and sealift for the first brigade of the Rapid Deployment Forces of which so much is made will not exist before 1985; that for the first division will not come into being quite before 1987 (besides which, the force level is inadequate).

How do we propose to cope in the first half of the decade before this new capability comes into being? How does the administration propose to relate our capabilities to our new commitments? Within two weeks of announcing the Carter Doctrine, the President acknowledged that we alone could not defend the vital Persian Gulf. Who then will join us? How can they help? What is our strategy? What forces will be available near the area for its defense? How can our current military establishment defend NATO, much less save distant allies? Why should we be surprised if threatened countries shy away from our protection?

These shortcomings, in my view, reflect the administration's profound ambivalence about the role of power in the world. Too many of its officials give the impression of feeling ashamed of American power and being fearful of military strength. They seem to operate on the premise that there is a guilt we must expiate rather than values we should defend.

Yet we cannot avoid the responsibilities that our power and principles confer upon us. Abdication will not purify us; it only creates a vacuum that will send to their destruction those who rely on us. At some point prudence turns into weakness which tempts danger; the ostentatious renunciation of force has the paradoxical consequence of magnifying risks. The fate of those who have fallen under Communist rule since 1975 makes clear that such hesitations can no longer parade under the banner of superior morality. At first the price for our ambivalence will be paid by others; in time— and fearfully—it will be paid by us.

The Geopolitical Balance

This brings me to my second concern: the geopolitical balance. By this I mean the alignments and assessments that determine whether moderates friendly to us, or radicals hostile to us, dominate key regions; whether our alliances are vital or sliding towards lassitude. It determines whether peaceful solutions of problems like the Arab-Israeli dispute or Southern Africa are possible, or whether the radical tide or Communist proxy intervention dooms all prospects of moderation and progress.

This geopolitical balance is measured partly by intangibles—by whether friends of the United States believe they have a secure future; by whether they have confidence in our ability to aid them against challenges and deter outside threats to regional security; by whether, indeed, they will even risk engaging in self-defense—as illustrated by Pakistan's refusal of our offer of military aid.

And it depends as well on *our* ability to perceive trends and dangers *before* they become overwhelming. A statesman must act on judgments about the future that cannot be proved true when they are made. When the scope for action is greatest, the knowledge on which to base such action is often least; when certain knowledge is at hand, the scope for creative action has often disappeared.

In 1936, the movement of one French division could have dissuaded Hitler from his march into the Rhineland. If France had done so, the world might still be arguing today whether Hitler was only a misunderstood nationalist or really a maniac bent on world domination. By 1941 everyone knew that Hitler was a maniac bent on world domination—but the world paid for its insistence on psychological certainty with millions of lives.

We face, I would submit, a similar challenge from the Soviet Union—not because they are necessarily implementing a timetable for world conquest but in the sense that incremental challenges not resisted will lead inexorably to greater challenges, even if the Soviets are only exploiting opportunities that come their way. This was precisely the issue when Soviet-supported Cuban troops occupied Angola, intervened in Ethiopia, sponsored two invasions of Zaire, and established a base in South Yemen; when there were two Communist coups in Afghanistan; and when finally the Soviet Army occupied that unhappy country. The problem was compounded and partly reflected by the collapse, for whatever reason, of a friendly government in Iran, which for 37 years had been a major ally of the United States and had in turn been an important bulwark of other moderate forces in the entire region. This development is a major cause of the slowdown of the Mideast peace process, as moderates like Egypt, Israel, and Jordan feel increasingly isolated, threatened, and constrained. The increasing climate of insecurity in the Persian Gulf affects not only political decisions but economic decisions, including OPEC's behavior on oil prices.

Four years ago, after the Senate vote cutting off aid to Angola, I warned [on Feb. 12, '76] that the Soviet/Cuban military intervention in Angola was the beginning of "a pattern" which, if unresisted, "would have the gravest consequences for peace and stability, and it is one which the United States treats with indifference only at the risk of buying graver crises at higher cost later on." Since then Soviet arms, Soviety proxy troops, Soviet friendship treaties, and outright Soviet intervention have determined the outcome of far too many local upheavals in the world's political alignments.

Precariously situated countries in the Middle East see the Soviet-supported Cuban advance coming through Africa to Ethiopia right across the Red Sea. They observe a Soviet base in South Yemen threatening the Arabian peninsula; they see Soviet-armed guerrillas invading Morocco, a traditional friend and moderate government; they see a Soviet arms depot in Libya—a precursor of future interventions in Africa and the Middle East. To them the Soviet invasion of Afghanistan now—coming eighteen months after an unopposed Communist coup in Kabul—overshadows the Persian Gulf like the northern arm of a great pincer. They observe Vietnam swallowing Cambodia and seeking hegemony over Southeast Asia under the protection of a Soviet friendship treaty. They notice that India and Pakistan are *both* vying for Soviet favor. Even in the Western Hemisphere they see radical upheavals rending Central America and the Caribbean, buttressed by a small Soviet combat force in Cuba. And they see no effective resistance.

This has its inevitable effect, which is to accelerate the demoralization of all moderate allies, driving friends toward neutralism and neutrals toward radicalism. The administration has explained certain of its actions as an effort to win the approbation and allegiance of the Third World countries. But the Conference of the Non-aligned Nations in Havana last September demonstrated that such a policy was built on quicksand. Never has the Conference passed such stridently anti-American, such unabashedly pro-Soviet resolutions, shocking even such a pillar of the non-aligned movement as President Tito. The radicalism of many Third World countries cannot be moderated by a more "understanding" American posture; they object to our existence or social structure, not to our policies. And the closer we attempt to approach toward them, the more they are likely to move further away from us simply to maintain their ideological purity.

Even with the less radical Third World countries—and they are still the majority—the issue is misconceived if put in terms of approbation and allegiance. For hardly any of the countries immediately threatened *prefers* the Soviet system. Their problem is the pressure they face from outside military force or internal subversion, the menace of radical groups flaunting their implacable ideological hatred of America, undermining the balance of power even when they are not financed, armed, and trained by the Soviet bloc—as they often are.

Somewhere, somehow, the United States must show that it is capable of rewarding a friend or penalizing an opponent. It must be made clear, after too long an interval, that our allies benefit from association with us and our enemies suffer. It is a simpleminded proposition perhaps, but for a great power it is the prerequisite, indeed the definition of an effective foreign policy.

The Attitude Towards Domestic Change

Thirdly, what should be our attitude to the process of domestic change in the world? The administration contends that by demonstrating our moral values and concern for human rights—if necessary by condemning our own previous actions—we will gain the approbation of mankind and thus outflank the Soviets.

Reality is more complex. It is true that American foreign policy must be grounded in the humane values of our people and of our democratic tradition. We would be neither effective nor faithful to ourselves if we sought to defend every status quo in an age of upheavals.

The problem, however, is to relate this truism to the national interest of the United States in concrete situations. It is a hard fact, but true, that some societies whose security is vital to us—particularly in the Persian Gulf—are governed by authoritarian conservative regimes. In the West constitutional democracy resulted from an evolution extending over centuries. Forcefeeding the process in developing societies is not impossible, but it has the paradoxical result of involving us in permanent global intervention at the precise moment when we have supposedly learnt our limits in the aftermath of the Vietnam experience.

At the same time we have dismantled the intelligence capability on which such interventionism would realistically depend. Ironically, many of those who have decried covert intelligence activities are urging a policy of *overt* intervention far more intrusive than was ever imagined in what current mythology pictures as the "bad old days."

Iran should teach us that humane values are not necessarily served by the overthrow of conservative regimes. If we encourage upheavals without putting in their place a moderate democratic alternative, a foreign policy conducted in the name of justice and human rights will wind up by making the world safe for anti-American radicalism. We will see new governments not only hostile to us but even more brutal toward human rights. All this tends to compound the geopolitical disintegration I have described earlier.

The acceleration of radical trends in the world, abetted by our policies, is visible to all. Nicaragua is often cited as a model of the new enlightenment. But while it is too early to pass a final judgment, one is uneasy when the latest human rights report of the State Department lists 400 summary executions and the holding of 7200 political prisoners in the six months of the new regime. And a Sandinista delegation visiting Moscow in March applauded the Soviet invasion of Afghanistan and condemned what it called "the campaign launched by imperialist and reactionary forces . . . to undermine the unalienable right of the Democratic Republic of Afghanistan's people . . . to go the way of progressive transformation."

Moreover, each new upheaval tends to start a rockslide. In the wake of Nicaragua, radical Marxist anti-American forces are gaining in El Salvador; Castroite elements are already implanted in Jamaica and Grenada and beginning the assault in Guatemala. With such currents sweeping Central America and the Caribbean, are we identifying with the wave of the future, or are we abetting our own progressive isolation and irrelevance? Will Mexico in self-defense not be driven towards radicalism and anti-Americanism by forces we encouraged but did not know how to channel?

Similar trends exist, of course, in the Persian Gulf and the Middle East. If improved judicial procedures were a main concern of Khomeini's revolution, he has kept it well hidden—with 700 executions and "thousands" of political prisoners, according to the State Department report, to say nothing of the illegal detention of our own diplomats. And how do we relate our human rights professions to the defense of our remaining friends in that vital area, most of whose domestic procedures fall short of our standards? Is it surprising that the few remaining moderate regimes are confused and apprehensive? Unless we get our priorities straight, external pressures will accelerate internal upheavals and produce a growing sense of insecurity and a growing trend of dissociation from the United States. Where would we be in the Middle East but for the miracle of Sadat's greatness?

Previous administrations perhaps showed too little sensitivity to the problem of domestic change. We do need a concept of change to which moderate democratic humane forces can rally. But currently there is entirely too much insouciance about a process that could easily engulf us. In too many parts of the world, we are losing our power to influence events for either good or ill. We live in a more hostile world today, in a weakened position, and the beginning of wisdom is to stop pretending that we are better off now because we have made obvious our desire to be universally loved.

US-Soviet Relations

Finally, let me address myself to the current crisis in US-Soviet relations.

In the age of thermonuclear weapons and intercontinental missiles, the interaction between the two superpowers must always be a central concern of American foreign policy. On this relationship depend the prospects for peace, our security and survival, and the hopes of the whole world for a better future.

Our relationship with Moscow is inherently ambiguous. Ideology implies an ineradicable conflict; nuclear weaponry compels coexistence. Geopolitical rivalry produces inevitable tension; military technology necessitates the peaceful solution of outstanding issues. How to achieve both peace *and* justice, how to prevent the fear of nuclear war from turning into nuclear blackmail, is a central challenge for American statesmanship.

Coexistence with the Soviet Union has always raised moral dilemmas for Americans. Indeed its dilemmas delayed our establishment of diplomatic relations with the USSR for over 16 years after the Bolshevik Revolution. And the same ambivalence persists. Today, liberals fear the military build-up and geopolitical vigilance that are the only basis for a secure relationship with the USSR; conservatives are uneasy lest the very fact of negotiation with the Soviet leaders erode all moral dividing lines, sapping the West's will to resist and our public's support for the necessary level of defense.

This explains why we have lacerated ourselves for decades in a debate over whether "containment" or "detente" or something else should be the goal of our policy toward the

Soviet Union. Those two concepts have indeed become epithets. In reality, a sensible long-term policy needs elements of both. We get into difficulty precisely when we misstate our alternatives.

It is no accident that an administration that three years ago proclaimed its emancipation from "the inordinate fear of Communism" allegedly afflicting its predecessors has brought us to an historic low point in our relationship with the Soviet Union. An administration more emotionally, even sentimentally devoted to arms control than any other, that proudly proclaimed that arms control could stand on its own feet without linkage to other issues, now finds its SALT treaty stymied—perhaps for that very reason. No doubt the principal fault is the Kremlin's insatiable tendency to exploit every strategic opportunity. There can be no coexistence while the Soviet Union presses to the margins of the tolerable and often beyond.

But it seems to me also true that we have confused the Soviet leaders by inconsistent pronouncements and unpredictable reactions. Erratic shifts in our policy, whatever their reason—whether from one administration to another, or within the term of one administration, or from the tug of war between Congress and the Executive—run the risk of evaporating the restraints operating on Soviet conduct.

This administration has in the space of a few years repudiated the SALT position of the previous administration and then returned to its basic framework two months later; we cancelled the neutron bomb and a year later pushed theater nuclear weapons; we proclaimed that the Persian Gulf needed no policeman and then announced a doctrine for its defense; we asserted the importance of Pakistan to the security of the area, then put forward a program incompatible with our stated objective, and finally dropped the entire project. We repeatedly rejected "linkage," which would have made progress in areas in which the Soviets had a stake—such as trade or SALT—dependent on Soviet restraint in exploiting tensions. This produced the spectacle that arms control proceeded while Soviet proxy forces moved into Ethiopia, while Soviet bases were established in South Yemen, while a first Communist coup took place in Afghanistan in 1978, and while a Soviet brigade was discovered in Cuba. And when Soviet troops moved to the Khyber Pass, we suddenly rediscovered linkage with a vengeance.

The essence of a strategic view is to see the interconnection of events, and the trend of events. Yet we have been unwilling to resist the seemingly marginal encroachments that cumulatively now amount to a major erosion of the free world's security. Paradoxically, by our acquiescence in the initial stages, the Soviets may even have felt misled when we later suddenly reacted—as we finally did after Afghanistan.

This American hesitation is not just the product of liberal inhibitions about intervention inherited from the Vietnam experience. Some American conservatives, too, at times seem more interested in building Fortress America and in patriotic rhetoric than in efforts to resist Soviet adventures overseas. This last was painfully evident in the Angola debate of 1975.

Every American should support the retaliatory steps announced by the President since January toward the Soviet Union—the deferral of SALT, the grain embargo, restriction on access to high technology, the Olympic boycott. These were the minimal response to Soviet aggression, but they are only reflex reactions; they do not constitute a strategy.

The administration has been rightly disappointed in the conduct of many of our allies, in particular the Europeans. It is indeed dismaying that the industrial countries that are more threatened than we by the turmoil in the Persian Gulf are reluctant to accept the risks of a forward policy against the Soviet Union. The Western Alliance will surely be jeopardized by the new theory of "division of labor" by which the Europeans seek to retain the benefits of a relaxation of tensions while we assume all the burdens and risks of resisting Soviet expansionism.

Nevertheless, our allies also have grounds for concern. Their hesitation and reluctance are not an accident. They rightly complain of a failure of consultation. They have been exposed to the same vacillations and cacophony of voices I have described with respect to East-West relations. They therefore wonder how long we will stick to our latest proclaimed course. If we want allies to gear their policies to ours, they must be able to comprehend not only the immediate punitive steps, but the long-term direction and thrust of our policy. Are we acting now in order to punish the Soviet Union for an individual act, after which we will resume the previous rhetoric and style? Or have we truly undertaken a new policy of firmness? Can our allies make sense of a new doctrine that generates additional commitments but *no* new forces? Are we committing ourselves to a long-term strategy that our allies can understand, that our Congress and public will sustain, and that will be carried out by the leadership groups of both parties regardless of who is victorious in November? And what is that strategy?

These questions must be answered, lest the Alliance wind up with empty posturing everywhere: on our side defiance unrelated to concept, in Europe accommodation drifting toward Finlandization.

At the same time, while I favor greater firmness and augmented defense, I view them not as ends in themselves but as the foundation of a new strategy of East-West diplomacy. We must never forget the lesson of World War II, when the democracies failed to maintain the balance of power and thereby invited aggression. But neither can we risk ignoring the lesson of World War I, when a war broke out *despite* the existence of a military balance, when statesmen lost control over their military planning and shortsighted posturing allowed an apparently minor crisis to escalate into a cataclysm that no leader intended or knew how to stop.

Some object to any negotiation with the Soviet Union, on the ground that it leads to euphoria or appeasement. I cannot accept the view that any serious dialogue with the Soviet Union must produce our moral disarmament. An attitude of rhetorical recalcitrance guarantees that we will be driven to negotiations in the worst circumstances, with our country torn apart by a debate over our "intransigence" and our allies buffeted by domestic assaults portraying America as the cause of world tensions. Our people surely understand the moral difference between tyranny and freedom and the necessity of both strength and survival; to maintain the proper balance is the task of leadership.

So let us not debate whether we should negotiate, but on what terms. Let us define an agenda that is neither sentimental nor bellicose, but is geared to the necessities of peace in our age. Let us articulate our own purposes, and not be driven into negotiations by the inevitable Soviet peace offensive. Let us transcend the labels of liberal and conservative as far as our foreign policy is concerned. They neither explain nor illuminate our necessities. We should spell out a position to which our people and our allies can repair, and negotiate at our own pace and on our own agenda.

In the thermonuclear age, it is simply too dangerous for the two superpowers not to be in contact. A stable long-term future requires, first, an American commitment to restore the balance of power; second, a perception that actions in different spheres and different parts of the world are linked in reality whatever one's theoretical aversion to "linkage;" together with, third, a willingness to settle outstanding issues on the basis of concreteness and reciprocity, not atmospheric goodwill.

After our election, whoever is in office should be prepared to open a dialogue with the USSR. But we must learn the lessons of the past. The greatest threat to peace is the Soviet tendency to exploit every tension for unilateral gain, undermining the security of free peoples. This must be stopped—even in the Soviet interest; the American people will not be defeated without noticing it, and when we react we shall resist—increasing the danger of war. Our goal in East-West diplomacy must be to determine what Soviet intentions are and spell out the limits of acceptable conduct. The era of proxy forces, military pressures, and encouragement of terrorists must be ended; it is incompatible with relaxation of tensions with the United States and must be shown to be so.

It is surely within America's capacity to establish the penalties and incentives to affect Soviet decisions and bring some measure of stability to the East-West relationship. We must avoid the temptation to identify progress with good personal relations or seek release in largely atmospheric gestures. While the men in the Kremlin do not mind playing on Western preconceptions that identify diplomacy with warm personal relations, they really do not know how to deal with a sentimental American policy. In the jungle of Soviet politics, no Soviet leader can justify conciliatory or self-denying policies toward the outside world except by stressing that such actions will eventually serve some Soviet aims or are necessary to avoid jeopardizing Soviet interests. It is up to us to establish these realities by our own purposeful, consistent conduct.

If progress is possible towards a code of restraint, we should be prepared to resume the SALT process. In my view we would be well advised, if and when we return to the negotiating table, to aim at a *new* SALT agreement to run for an extended period, say 10–15 years, that would limit the *next* cycle of weapons developments. In this case, we could also broaden the negotiation to include Soviet theater nuclear weapons, as well as planned NATO deployments, in consultation with our allies.

But I cannot stress sufficiently that all of this presupposes reliable assurances of an end to the current Soviet geopolitical offensive. If these are unobtainable we will have no choice except confrontation—and we only weaken our position by implying, as is so often done, that an arms race might work against our interests or that a confrontation would present us with greater problems than our adversary.

Conclusion

Let me conclude, in other words, on a hopeful note. Almost all the problems outlined here are self-inflicted. We should keep in mind that we alone have twice the Gross National Product of the Soviet Union and, with our allies, five times the Gross National Product of the Soviet Union. If we are lagging militarily behind, it is through a lack of will, not of resources; it is within our capacity to rectify it.

We should remember that the Soviet system of government has never managed a legitimate succession. There have only been four leaders in the entire history of the Soviet Union in over 60 years. Two died in office, the third was replaced by a palace coup, and the fourth is determined to return to the earlier tradition.

Given the decrepitude of the current leadership, such a system cannot represent the wave of the future. Nor has any planned economy ever been able to match the performance of a market economy. Whether one compares Czechoslovakia and Austria, East and West Germany, North and South Korea, market economies have invariably outstripped socialist models. Stagnation seems inherent in the Soviet system. The Kremlin's dilemma is that one cannot run a modern economy with total planning, but it may also be impossible to run the Soviet system without such planning.

Two partly contradictory trends are thus involved. We face a period of maximum danger in the next five years, while the military balance is still tipping against us and the cycle of local revolutions is playing itself out. After that, the certainty is that Soviet domestic problems will mount, and our new defense programs can restore the equilibrium. But before then, Soviet reformers and Soviet conservatives may be able to unite on only one set of goals: to secure their international environment brutally and urgently before reassessing their domestic system. It is within our power to close off the avenue of adventurism, but the time is growing short. As is often the case, the seemingly boldest course is really the safest; procrastination will only prolong and thereby magnify our danger.

Therefore, as soon as possible we must restore the balance of military power. But once we do so, we face an historic opportunity. Let us make clear that we are ready for a more constructive future: a world free of the danger of nuclear blackmail; a world in which mankind's desire for peace does not become a weapon in the hand of the most ruthless but is allied to the determination of the just; a world of hope and of progress. With all our travail we remain the most fortunate people in the world: because we have the means, if we have the will, to solve our own problems. History will not do our work for us. But history tells us that we can help ourselves.

STRENGTHENING SINO-AMERICAN RELATIONS[1]

WALTER F. MONDALE[2]

Vice President Walter Mondale arrived in China for a week's visit on August 13, 1979, as a return gesture for Deputy Prime Minister Deng Xiaoping's visit to the United States seven months earlier. In a series of meetings characterized as "extremely productive and friendly," Mondale conferred at length with China's two top leaders: Deputy Premier Deng Xiaoping and Communist Party Chairman Hua Kuofeng. Their agenda included: trade between the two nations, extending credit to China, expanding the cultural exchange, the Cambodian situation, and US help in developing China's hydro-electric power.

At 3:40 p.m. (China time), August 27, 1979, Vice President Walter Mondale delivered a message from President Carter to a standing audience of 800 at Peking University, and to a larger radio and television audience. The address called attention to the fact that the Vice President was "the first American political figure to speak directly to the citizens of the People's Republic of China."

The crowded schedule of events that preceded the speech give some indication of the pressure that the Vice President was under. A. Denis Cliff, Assistant to the Vice President for National Security Affairs, describes the day as follows:

> The Vice President had begun his Monday schedule in Beijing with two hours of talks with Vice Premier Deng Xiaoping. Following those talks he had continued discussions with other Chinese officials including Vice Premier Fang Yi at the Diaoyutai Guest House, where the Vice President and his party were staying. The Vice President arrived at Beijing University at 3:30 p.m.

---

[1] Delivered at Peking University (Bei-Da) to students and faculty and also via radio and television, at 3:40 P.M., August 27, 1979. Title supplied by editor. Quoted by permission.
[2] For biographical note, see Appendix.

where he was met by Zhou Peiyuan, President of the University, and other University officials. There was a brief reception at the University's Reception House. Following that the Vice President and his hosts proceeded on foot to the Beijing University auditorium where he delivered the address (letter to editor, April 22, 1980).

In studying the speech, it should be remembered that it was to be scrutinized by the leadership of the People's Republic of China and would be regarded as an official statement of US foreign policy and intentions. Therefore, work must have been done on it not only by Mondale's staff, but also the US State Department. Obviously, the speech was primarily a gesture of good will, and from a rhetorical point of view, the situation controlled the content. Mondale assured the Chinese that "a strong and secure and modernizing China is ... in the American interest in the decade ahead," and reasoned that "despite the sometimes profound differences between our two systems, we are committed to joining with you to advance our many parallel strategic and bilateral interests."

I am honored to appear before you. And I bring you the warm greetings and the friendship of the President of the United States and the American people.

For an American of my generation to visit the People's Republic of China is to touch the pulse of modern political history. For nearly three decades our nations stood separate and apart. But the ancient hunger for community unites humanity. It urges us to find common ground.

As one of your poets wrote over a thousand years ago, "We widen our view three hundred miles by ascending one flight of stairs." We are ascending that flight of stairs together.

Each day we take another step. This afternoon, I am privileged to be the first American political figure to speak directly to the citizens of the People's Republic of China.

And no setting for that speech could be more symbolic of our relationship than this place of new beginnings. The history of modern China is crystallized in the story of Beijing University and the other distinguished institutions you represent. At virtually every turning point in the 20th century China, Bei-Da has been the fulcrum.

Sixty years ago, it was at Bei-Da that the May 4th movement began, launching an era of unprecedented intellectual ferment. It inaugurated an effort to modernize Chinese culture and society. It established a new meeting ground for eastern and western cultures. And its framework of mutual respect sustains our own cultural cooperation today.

Forty-four years ago, Bei-Da was where the December 9th movement galvanized a student generation to resist external aggression. And its message of sovereignty and nonaggression underpins our own political cooperation today.

As China looks to the future, once again it is Bei-Da and your other research centers which are leading the drive toward "the four modernizations" [agriculture, science and technology, industry, and defense]. And the closeness of your development goals to our own interests will provide the basis for our continuing economic cooperation.

Today, we find our two nations at a pivotal moment. We have normalized our relations. The curtain has parted; the mystery is being dispelled. We are eager to know more about one another, to share the texture of our daily lives, to forge the human bonds of friendship.

That is a rich beginning. But it is only a beginning.

A modern China taking its place in the family of nations is engaged in a search not only for friendship, but also for security and development. An America deepening its relations with China does so not only out of genuine sentiment, and not only out of natural curiosity. It does so out of the same combination of principle and self-interest that is the engine of mature relations among all modern states.

Our job today is to establish the basis for an enduring relationship tomorrow. We could not have set that task without our friendship. But we cannot accomplish it with friendship alone.

On behalf of President Carter, this is the message I carry to the people of China—a message about America, its purposes in the world, and our hopes for our relations with you.

The Americans are historically confident people. Our politics are rooted in our values. We cherish our fundamental beliefs in human rights, and compassion, and social justice. We believe that our democratic system institutionalizes those values. The opportunities available to our citizens are incomparable. Our debates are vigorous and open. And the differences we air among ourselves—whether on strategic nuclear policy or on energy—are signs of our society's enduring strength.

My country is blessed with unsurpassed natural resources. Moreover, we also have unparalleled human resources—workers and farmers and scientists and engineers and industrialists and financiers. With their genius we are able to transform our natural assets into abundance—not only for ourselves, but for the world.

Of course we face unsolved problems. But the high goals we set for ourselves—and our determination to meet them—are measures of our national spirit. In that striving, in that restless pursuit of a better life, we feel a special affinity for the people of modern China.

In the world community, the United States seeks international stability and peace. But we have no illusions about the obstacles we face. We know that we live in a dangerous world. And we are determined to remain militarily prepared. We are fashioning our defenses from the most advanced technology anywhere. We have forged alliances in Europe and Asia which grow stronger every year. Together with our Japanese and Western allies, we will ensure that our investment in security is equal to the task of ensuring peace—as we have for thirty years.

But we want to be more than a firm and reliable partner in world affairs. We also believe in a world of diversity. For Sino-American relations, that means that we respect the distinctive qualities which the great Chinese people contribute to our relationship. And despite the sometimes profound differences between our two systems, we are committed to joining with you to advance our many parallel strategic and bilateral interests.

Thus any nation which seeks to weaken or isolate you in world affairs assumes a stance counter to American interests.

This is why the United States normalized relations with your country, and that is why we must work to broaden and strengthen our new friendship.

We must press forward now to widen and give specificity to our relations. The fundamental challenges we face are to build concrete political ties in the context of mutual security . . . to establish broad cultural relations in a framework of genuine equality . . . and to forge practical economic bonds with the goal of common benefit.

As we give substance to our shared interests, we are investing in the future of our relationship. The more effectively we advance our agenda, the more bonds we build between us—the more confident we can be that our relationship will endure.

And so what we accomplish today lays the groundwork for the decade ahead. The 1980s can find us working together—and working with other nations—to meet world problems. Enriching the global economy, containing international conflicts, protecting the independence of nations: these goals must also be pursued from the perspective of our bilateral relationship. The deeper the relationship, the more successful that world-wide pursuit will be.

That is the agenda President Carter has asked me to come to the People's Republic of China to pursue. That is the principal message President Carter has asked me to bring to you. It is the agenda we share for the future.

In the eight months since normalization, we have witnessed the rapid expansion of Sino-American relations.

We have reached a settlement on claims/assets and signed the trade agreement. Trade between our countries is expanding. American oil companies are helping you explore China's offshore oil reserves. Joint commissions on Sino-American economic relations and on scientific and technical exchange have been established. We have exchanged numerous governmental delegations, including the visits of many heads of our respective ministries and departments. And the flow of people between our two countries is reaching new heights.

We have gained a cooperative momentum. Together let us sustain and strengthen it.

For a strong and secure and modernizing China is also in the American interest in the decade ahead.

In agriculture, your continued development not only provides a better life for the Chinese people, it also serves our interests—for your gains in agriculture will increase limited world food supplies.

In trade, our interests are served by your expanding exports of natural resources and industrial products. And at the same time your interests are served by the purchases you can finance through those exports.

As you industrialize, you provide a higher standard of living for your people. And at the same time our interests are served—for this will increase the flow of trade, narrow the wealth gap between the developed and the developing world, and thus help alleviate a major source of global instability.

Above all, both our political interests are served by your growing strength in all fields—for it helps deter others who might seek to impose themselves on you.

Efforts in the 1920s and 1930s to keep China weak destabilized the entire world. For many years, China was a flash point of great power competition. But a confident China can contribute to the maintenance of peace in the region. Today, the unprecedented and friendly relations among China, Japan, and the United States bring international stability to Northeast Asia.

That is why deepening our economic, cultural, and political relations is so strategically important—not only for your security, but for the peace of the world community.

We are taking crucial steps to advance our economic relationship.

First, before the end of the year, President Carter will submit for the approval of the US Congress the trade agreement we reached with you. This agreement will extend "most favored nation" treatment to China. And its submission is not linked to any other issue.

Second, I will be signing an agreement on development of hydroelectric energy in the People's Republic of China. US Government agencies are now ready to help develop China's hydroelectric power on a compensatory basis.

Third, the United States is prepared to establish Export-Import Bank credit arrangements for the PRC on a case-by-case basis, up to a total of 2 billion (two thousand million) dollars over a five-year period. If the pace of development warrants it, we are prepared to consider additional credit arrangements. We have begun discussions toward this end.

Fourth, the Carter Administration this year will seek congressional authority to encourage American businesses to invest in China—by providing the guarantees and insurance of the Overseas Private Investment Corporation.

We also stand ready to work with the Chinese Government to reach textile, maritime, and civil aviation agreements in the shortest possible time.

As we advance our cultural relationship, universities will again be a crucial meeting-ground between Chinese and Americans, just as they were in an earlier era.

Today, gifted Chinese scholars study in America, and American scholars—many of whom I am delighted to see here today—study in China. That exchange inherits a distinguished tradition. On campuses all across the United States, Americans who lectured and studied in China in the 1930s and 1940s today are invigorating our own intellectual life—none of them with greater distinction than Professor John K. Fairbank, who honors us by joining my traveling party. At the same time, we are proud that Chinese scholars who studied American agronomy, engineering, and medicine have been able to contribute the skills they gained in our country to the progress of Chinese society.

It is a mutual relationship—a true reciprocity—we are now engaged in building. From us, you will learn aspects of science and technology. Our anthropologists and archeologists have tools to share with you as you explore your own past. American and Chinese social scientists and humanists have insights to offer each other—a fuller understanding of our respective institutions and values.

And so with your help, we intend to broaden our horizons. Chinese researchers pioneer in key areas, from medical burn therapy to earthquake prediction—and we want to learn these skills from you. Where the progress of science requires global cooperation—in astronomy, in oceanography, in meteorology—our common efforts can benefit the world. And our social scientists and humanists have hardly begun to share your understanding of history, of social change, and of human potential.

Strong bilateral relations serve our strategic interests. Through them, both of us can foster the world community we seek—a world that respects diversity and welcomes constructive change.

Today, there are 162 nations in the world, most of them poor. Eighty percent of the world's population live in developing countries. Every day, people in these nations are lifting their heads to demand independence and justice. Every day, efforts by rulers to oppress their people are meeting increasing resistance. Governments are coming to understand not only the necessity, but also the fundamental wisdom and decency of protecting the rights of their people through law.

When political power is more equitably shared within nations: When that power shifts from the few to the many among nations; when an era of colonialism gives way to a more just international order—these changes deserve worldwide support.

In the last few years, as the preeminent military and economic power in the world, the United States faced a fundamental choice. Were we to resist those winds of change, attaining our national security by defending the status quo? Were we to collude with a few other countries in an effort to dominate the world? Or were we to welcome change, to make the necessary adjustments, and to help shape a more just world order?

Let there be no doubt about the choice my country has made. The United States believes that any effort by one country to dominate another is doomed to failure. Neither by relying exclusively on an increasing stock of arms, nor by direct or indirect military intervention, can any nation hope to attain lasting security. On the contrary, nations which embark on that course will find themselves increasingly isolated and vulnerable.

And nothing more vividly demonstrates our belief in those principles than the normalization of Sino-American relations. Normalization signals our understanding that American security in the years ahead will be attained not by maintaining the status quo; not by colluding for purposes of domination; but by fostering a world of independent nations with whom we can build positive relations.

That is the world community we seek. It is a vision of diversity, of constructive ties—and above all, of peace.

In a world that hopes to find a new energy source, peace is essential. In a world that aims to eliminate hunger and disparities in wealth, global equilibrium is vital. In a world that is working to eradicate communicable diseases and to safeguard our environment, international cooperation is crucial.

To secure that peace, to maintain that equilibrium, to promote that cooperation—the United States is totally committed.

During the visit to the United States by vice premier Deng and Madame Zhuo in January, President Carter said this: "We've not entered this new relationship for any short-term gains. We have a long-term commitment to a world community of diverse ... and independent nations. We believe that a strong and secure China will play a cooperative part in developing that type of world community."

I would like to underscore that point. Anyone who seeks to understand America is invariably drawn back to the idea of diversity. The United States is a nation of immigrants, all of whom contribute to our society their distinct talents and traditions.

The American people find their common heritage not in a single bloodline, not in thousands of years of shared national history, but in their shared ideals. And we have a profound faith in the very diversity that shapes us. We value tolerance and pluralism and mutual respect.

We aim to honor those same principles in the conduct of our foreign policy in the decade of the 80s. For Sino-American relations, that does not mean we will always agree.

But in a world that respects diversity, countries as different as the United States and China can work side by side toward the common goals. Together, we can enrich our two cultures, strengthen our two economies, build better lives for both our peoples. And together, we can help stabilize the world community—fostering respect for diversity, and standing firmly opposed to intolerance and domination.

Last month, China and the United States joined many other nations in Geneva to confront the agony of the Indo-Chinese refugees. The enormity of their human tragedy defies the imagination. In a world that seeks to alleviate such suffering—suffering that transcends national boundaries—the way of conscience is the way of common cause.

Today the world watches us. In a sense, we are testing whether a developed nation and a developing nation—each with different traditions, each with different systems—can build a broad, enduring, constructive relationship. Certainly there will be serious barriers to overcome. But if we can work together, future generations will thank us. If we fail, not only will our children suffer: the entire world will feel the consequences.

Diversity and stability are not new themes in Sino-American relations. President Roosevelt once said this:

"It is to the advantage—and not to the disadvantage—of other nations, when any nation becomes stable and prosperous, able to keep the peace within its own borders, and strong enough not to invite aggression from without. We heartily hope for the progress of China. And so far as by peaceable and legitimate means we are able, we will do our part toward furthering that progress."

It was a bright vision three generations ago—and subsequent events only postponed the fulfillment of its promise. As we look to the future, let us resolve to rekindle the light of its insight.

DE-MYSTIFYING ANTI-AMERICANISM[1]
CHARLES W. BRAY III [2]

The central problem seems ... to be whether it is
possible to reconcile the preservation of cultural differences all people feel, and which most people cherish,
with some new model of modernization, neither Western
libertarian nor Marxist, a model which might produce
material prosperity without alienating or destroying traditional cultures.

In his examination of anti-Americanism, prevalent in the world
today, Charles W. Bray III, Deputy Director of The International
Communication Agency, discussed the dilemma that the United
States and other major powers face in dealing with the Third
World, "most particularly in Muslim countries." At 10 a.m. on
January 17, 1980, he addressed 60 students enrolled in the Foreign
Policy Semester, conducted by the College of Public Affairs of
American University in Washington, D.C.

His speech was designed to give a wider view of the problems
that the United States has encountered in Iran or, in his words, to
"de-mystify anti-Americanism." Pointing out that adverse views of
American policy and distrust of American motives are often mistaken for anti-Americanism, he examines the underlying causes of
resentment and hate implicit in anti-Americanism.

The development of Bray's argument follows a problem-solu-
tion order. About one half of the speech centers around establish-
ing the problem that "The frictions between traditional identity
and technological progress are agonizing." The solution, located in
the second half, comes in the form of an answer to the question:
"What then are the tentative conclusions to be drawn from this
complex mix of envy, emulation, dislocation, rage, policy conflicts?" In his four part answer, he advocates accommodation and
patience, and more knowledge and understanding of other cultures.

What interests me at this juncture is whether we understand—as a people—the nature of the world we are condemned by history to help manage.

[1] Delivered to a seminar of the Foreign Policy Semester, conducted by the College of Public Affairs, American University, Washington, D.C., 10 A.M., January 17,
1980.

[2] For biographical note, see Appendix.

Since early November the endless chants of "Death to America" emanating from crowds at our embassy in Tehran and the attacks on our properties in Islamabad, Tripoli and elsewhere have led many of us to believe that anti-American feeling is rampant at least in the Middle East and perhaps by extension elsewhere in the world.

How accurate is this picture? And why does it seem that we have become the villains of the international community?

I should like to try to address these questions this morning. My goal is to de-mystify anti-Americanism.

The phenomenon exists. It is real. It has important effects. But our national interests require the clearest understanding of what is at issue, lest our visceral reactions, our policies, our objectives lead us in false directions. The events in Iran have riveted our attention lately, but they have also clouded our memories. Feelings of resentment toward this country are not new. They have been part of the international landscape at least since the end of World War II. Resentment has grown in direct proportion to our influence in the world; indeed, resentment of the rich and powerful is as much a part of the life of nations as it is of the life of individuals. Our existence guarantees that we should be resented. We cannot escape it and it is idle to try.

Familiar as it is, however, anti-Americanism has never been easy to define. The phrase may not even be useful for explaining events in Iran or elsewhere in that region. "Anti-Americanism" defined simply as dislike—even hatred—of all things American, may preclude our understanding of other more important realities, inimical as they may be.

The body of world opinion about the United States is neither overwhelmingly negative nor consistent in its content. Indeed, despite the mob violence and the attacks on the United States, this country continues to be a source of hope and an object of esteem to a remarkable extent around the world. These statements derive in part from my own observation of many foreign societies, in part from research findings by our agency on what people believe about America in the world today.

From a review of the available research, we have found no hard evidence that a major change in opinion about the United States has occurred in the developed world. Instead, there has been—as a constant fact of the last two decades—strong, repeated, widespread evidence of general esteem and respect for this country. These views have persisted beyond specific events and overt acts of "anti-Americanism."

The most important finding of our review is that "anti-Americanism" usually mixes *general* feelings about the US—predominantly positive—with specific reactions to *specific* policy issues or to perceptions of the US and its military power, or distrust of our motives, or scepticism as to our reliability and so on.

On the specifics, attitudes are mixed. In 1972, for example, publics in 15 developed countries had a generally favorable view of us. In 13 of these same 15 countries, however, the general public had a largely negative opinion of our Vietnam policy. Adverse views of the US and adverse views of specific policies are different things; the point is that it is over-simplified and confusing to equate criticism of US policies with anti-Americanism.

The phenomenon of anti-Americanism in the Third World, and most particularly in Muslim countries, deserves special and careful analysis. The lack of data is a handicap, but possible explanations present themselves based on a close reading of events.

We like to assume that all good things are compatible: democracy and economic development go hand in hand; prosperity means peace and probably friendship. Life would be far easier if these things were true. But they may not be, and we are only now discovering this. Indeed, some of the current rage we see may be directed at the Western model of modernization itself; and by extension to the rapid change we as a nation epitomize.

The orthodox theories of development, both Marxist and Western libertarian, proceed from a shared assumption: development requires that modern economic and social organization replace traditional structures. Widely accepted in the US and elsewhere, this assumption encompasses, among other elements: industrialization in the economy; secularization in thought, personality, and communication; the development of "cosmopolitan attitudes;" and integration into the "world culture."

We have accepted the assumption despite its obvious flaw: that the elements of modernity—values, institutions, technological knowhow—could be transferred from the advanced West to the rest of the world without social, cultural or moral costs.

I think you will agree that when we look at the process of modernization in this manner, especially in light of Iran, it ignores some profoundly important phenomena, namely the role and persistence of traditional values.

If a country appeared to conform to the expected course of modernization, it was Iran. All of the accepted indicators of development pointed to this. But the case of Iran shows that the introduction of modernizing programs does not necessarily lead to a "withering away" of the significance—indeed the political role—of traditional values and religion. On the contrary, one effect of the agonies and dislocations of development may be to make religion more salient as a social and political force.

It is no accident that *The Christian Science Monitor* recently called the Ayatollah Khomeini and Pope John Paul II the "two most charismatic figures on earth." Both are religious leaders. Both are symbols, within the world's great monotheistic religions, of the deep-rooted certainties of the past. In earlier centuries these certitudes gave people strength, hope, and security. Today they provide familiar cultural and psychological guideposts in the face of rapid change. Out of this rage against modernization's tendency to engulf or destroy traditional values has come a search for identity, for uniqueness. Says Egyptian commentator Hamdi Fuad, "We can never be the same as you; we have to find the way to be us."

Parenthetically, Islam is not alone in experiencing a new attraction for uneasy souls contemplating the close of the 20th century. The West also has a sense of uncertainty about its moral and religious values. There is now underway a dra-

matic resurgence of Christian evangelicalism in our own
country. It, too, must in part reflect a reaction to the rapidity
of change, the great dislocation and traumatic events of the
1960s and early 1970s.

For some in the Third World, this renewed search for
identity has come to entail *at least* partial rejection of Western social and cultural influence. It does not necessarily mean
a rejection of modern technique, but of the idea that one has
to remake oneself into a faithful copy of its Western origina-
tors in order to put the technique to use. As another Egyptian
puts it, "If the sum total of Western culture is coming to me
as jeans, Coke, murder films, T-shirts, then this is what I
would reject."

There is a paradox. People are not prepared to turn their
backs on science and technology, or the benefits of better
health and longer lives; nor, on the other hand are they ready
to see their cultural identity submerged under a veneer of
technocratic civilization. A Malaysian has summed up the
problem well, "A serious mistake made by Western scholars,"
he says, "is to assume that all people who become educated
are necessarily going to be Westernized."

The frictions between traditional identity and technological progress are agonizing. There is a psychological dialectic
to be worked out. It will be deeply troubling to those involved. It will result in periodic explosions of rage. We will
be the objects of that rage as often as not. We represent that
which is simultaneously desired and disliked, that toward
which people strive and that which they fear may be unobtainable. We exert an hypnotic attraction, but we threaten
people's deepest identities. And there is almost nothing we or
they can do about it. The question it raises for all of us in the
International Communication Agency is whether we have ad-
equately recognized the power of these forces, analyzed their
implications for our communication programs—and whether
we have dug deeply enough in our efforts to describe the
roots of our own experience and accomplishments. Those
roots are in important respects religious and value centered.
Or have we focused too much on the surface manifestations of
our country?

This profound agonizing psychological and cultural dilemma is, of course, intensified by some straightforwardly different national interests and objectives. We support Israel's right to exist; that policy imperative is greater than our support for a Palestinian homeland. We cannot expect our policy to be welcomed in Muslim countries. We supported the Shah of Iran, in part for sound geopolitical reasons since Iran stands between the Soviet Union and the Persian Gulf, in part because for many years he was making an enlightened effort to bring his country the benefits of modernity. Those who suffered as a result—including the uprooted villager or the chauvinist male Muslim—have no great reason to be pro-American. Or a third example: we have sought to deny an essentially defenseless and humiliated Pakistan the right of access to the nuclear technology it believes central to its defense against India. This is not a policy calculated to win admirers in Pakistan. We adopted each of these policies for good reasons, but each has added a dash of fuel to an already explosive cultural problem.

The curiosity is not that the West in general, and the United States in particular, are the subject of rage—but that we remain so widely admired and respected, even an object of emulation among so many.

What then are the tentative conclusions to be drawn from this complex mix of envy, emulation, dislocation, rage, policy conflicts?

First, it should now be less easy to believe that as the Third World industrializes, it will adopt Western values wholesale at the expense of "outdated" traditional values. This was at best an oversimplification. It may be that there are some forces in human affairs which we simply cannot affect, but which have a life and logic of their own. It may also be that the closer we get to the roots of cultures—and here I refer to traditional and religious values—the less outside influences matter. Some problems in life cannot be solved; it cuts deeply against the American grain to acknowledge that fact, but it is no less a fact. We should accommodate to it at least in part.

Secondly, there seems no way to go back. Whatever the

West has done to the East—and in many cases it would be difficult to show that it was detrimental—it is now a fact of life. We must accept Oliver Wendell Holmes' statement that: "a man's mind, stretched to a new idea, never goes back to its original dimensions." We need not feel great guilt. Much of what has transpired in non-Western countries since independence reflects their desires—for industrialization, and modernization. We all underestimated the costs, and it is psychologically easier for them to blame us. So be it.

The central problem seems therefore to be whether it is possible to reconcile the preservation of cultural differences all people feel, and which most people cherish, with some new model of modernization, neither Western libertarian nor Marxist, a model which might produce material prosperity without alienating or destroying traditional cultures. It may prove to be that the values which lie beneath technology—give rise to it and support it—cannot be reconciled with societies in which religion is the great organizing principle for all of life. In that case, the choices will be agonizing.

Thirdly, no great power with a popular, hypnotic culture for export, an expansive economy, great military capacity, an attractive (and often inherently destabilizing) political philosophy, can expect to be the object of universal affection. We ought not to fret about that fact. We should focus, instead, on how we can comport ourselves in a way which advances our interests, the broad interests of the international community, and the interests of vulnerable cultures and societies, in the most broadly satisfactory and sensitive way. There is important work here for all of us, including those of us in the International Communication Agency.

At the same time, Iran and the surge of Islamic belief should make us realize that the gaps in our understanding of other societies may well be chasms. If we have learned that we must do our best to make ourselves understood abroad, we have also learned that we must do more to understand the complexities of the world in which we live. We are, or should be, agreed that we can no longer overwhelm our foreign problems simply by throwing our resources at them. It fol-

lows from this that we must live increasingly by our wits—
like most other societies. The preconditions to wit are information and judgement. In this context, it cannot be comforting to learn that a recent survey of high school seniors showed
40 percent believed Israel to be an Arab nation. If we are to
live by our wits then clearly there is a notable contribution
yet to be made to the sophistication and knowledge which
Americans bring to bear on their affairs with the rest of the
world.

It may be that Americans, both by temperament and
training, are ill-equipped to deal with a smaller, closer world.
We are thrown into contact and conflict with peoples whose
histories and motivations we hardly understand. Our language inadequacies, documented in the recently released *Report of the President's Commission on Foreign Language and
International Studies*, may betray a sense of moral superiority.

Finally, we fool ourselves if we view the Iranian experience as a freak accident. We will do better to recognize it as a
painful example of an important and widespread phenomenon: the instabilities which accompany the clash of the old
and the new, the cherished and the coveted.

The challenge is there. It is an urgent and compelling one.
Kurt Waldheim, Secretary General of the United Nations said
something rather arresting in a recent annual report. "Many
great civilizations have collapsed at the very height of their
achievement," he said, "because they were unable to analyze
their basic problems, to change direction, and to adjust to the
new situations which face them by concerting their wisdom
and strength."

Our own tradition is to meet change with noise, with disagreement, with intense debate—and from this to extract the
necessary adjustments. The challenge for us as public officials, and for all concerned with the fate of our country and
world peace, is to insure that the experiment continues, that
the debate is focused and productive, that our capacity for
change endures—and, not least of all, that we can adjust to
our new international situation by concerting our wisdom and
our strength.

THE UNITED STATES AND THE
COMING WORLD FOOD CRISIS[1]

JOHN H. SULLIVAN[2]

Hunger has been internationalized and turned into a
continuing global issue, transformed from a low-profile
moral imperative to a divisive and disruptive factor in
international relations. The most potentially explosive
force in the world today is the frustrated desire of poor
people to attain a decent standard of living. The anger,
despair and often hatred that result represent a real and
persistent threat to international order.

These statements are from the recent Preliminary Report of
the Presidential Commission on World Hunger (*Congressional
Record*, D. '79, p E6095). The Commission further warns, "A
major crisis of global food supplies appears likely within the next
twenty years unless steps are taken to facilitate a significant increase in food production in the developing countries." This stark
prediction serves as a fitting preface to the address that John H.
Sullivan, Assistant Administrator of the Bureau of Asia for International Development, delivered at the annual College of Agriculture Food Conference, University of Wisconsin in River Falls,
Wisconsin, one p.m. on April 26, 1979. The address served as an
introductory comment to a discussion session which Sullivan
shared with Abidur Rhamdn, economic minister of the Embassy of
The People's Republic of Bangladesh and Loyd Bailor of the Embassy of Sierra Leone. The audience consisted of undergraduate
and graduate students, faculty members, and community residents
and met in the auditorium of the Agriculture Science Building.

His presentation represents an expansion of the subject of
world malnutrition and food shortage by American leaders. For
other speeches on the same subject, the reader may be interested
in addresses by Henry A. Kissinger, Earl L. Butz, and Mark O.
Hatfield in *Representative American Speeches, 1974–1975* and

---

[1] Delivered at the annual College of Agriculture Food Conference, the University of Wisconsin-River Falls, 1 P.M., April 26, 1979. Quoted by permission.
[2] For biographical note, see Appendix.

those by Robert S. McNamara and John A. Hannah in the 1976–1977 edition.

The organization and content of this talk follow a traditional five-step plan (called a "motivated sequence"): attention, need (problem), solution, benefits, and appeal for action. The supporting material (evidence) is ample and graphic. The references to the Old Testament story of Joseph make a good beginning and closing.

Joseph, the Book of Genesis tells us, saved Egypt much agony when he forecast seven years of plenty to be followed by seven years of famine. For at the same time that he predicted the future, he also advised the Pharaoh on how to plan for it. Store up food, said Joseph, and the nation will not perish through the lean years. This foresight not only spared Egypt but left the country with enough corn to help neighboring countries survive the hard times.

Joseph's wisdom is as relevant—and critical—today as it was in Biblical times. Statistics indicate that these are fat years—years of relative agricultural plenty. Yet, the globe, which still holds large pockets of underfed people, is facing the prospect of greatly increased malnutrition as population growth outstrips agricultural production and food distribution remains inequitable. Moreover, a siege of unfavorable weather could plunge Third World countries into widespread famines.

Despite these prospects, the world is not following Joseph's example by preparing for the seemingly inevitable food crisis. Instead, many in the developing world are acting as if the problem is easing, that the fat years are here to stay.

This confidence is no where greater than in Asia. This year our newspapers are heralding record harvests there:

The subcontinent is in the midst of a record fourth consecutive bumper crop. Famine-prone *India* has experienced a 25 percent increase in food grain production since the disastrous flood of 1973–1974.

At the same time *Sri Lanka* has reduced its food imports to the lowest level in 30 years.

Last year's harvest was the best for *Bangladesh* since it became independent seven years ago.

South Korea, in East Asia, has become self-sufficient in rice.

For the first time, the *Philippines* has become a marginal rice exporter.

Burma has record surpluses of food.

Indonesia is showing a record low food deficit.

But does this good news also mean that the world has begun to turn the corner on famine or malnutrition? Or does the small print below the headlines indicate that this success is a temporary phenomenon?

I believe it is the latter—that good harvests notwithstanding we are faced with a growing food crisis.

To begin with, it is clear that despite optimum weather conditions agricultural production is barely apace with the growing needs of Asian countries. Since 1975, rice production on the Asian continent has increased approximately 15 percent and the yield per acre has gone up nearly 10 percent. Nevertheless, current estimates indicate an overall LDC [Less Developed Countries] grain deficit by 1990 of roughly 80 million tons. Asia, which contains about four-fifths of the populations of the lowest income LDCs, is expected to account for the major part of that shortfall.

The causes of this potential shortage basically are two:

First, there are more mouths to feed because of rapidly growing populations. Assuming UN medium variant population growth rates, between 75 and 90 percent of the increased demand for food in AID's [Agency for International Development] program countries in Asia throughout the remainder of this century will be attributable to increases in people.

Consider, for example, the country of Bangladesh, which is almost to the square mile the size of this state of Wisconsin. While Wisconsin has a population of about 4.7 million people, Bangladesh has 87 million people. And although Wisconsin's population is stable and likely to remain so, Bangladesh's population will virtually double by the year 2000 (about the time your kids are in grade school).

The second reason for the food shortage is, ironically

enough, development successes that have led to more money for developing people. Upper income groups spend relatively little of their additional income on agricultural commodities. Thus, if only the upper classes receive increased income, new demand for food is relatively small and usually for luxury foods, not staples. When poor people make more money, though, they spend most of it on basic foods. Of the income groups in India, the lowest 20 percent spends 60 percent of its new income on grain and some 85 percent on agricultural commodities.

"Put simply," says food expert John Mellor: "rapid growth in the income of the poor results in explosive growth in demand for food."

The case of Indonesia illustrates the degree to which the demand for food can increase. Its good harvests notwithstanding, Indonesia is still the largest importer of rice in the world. Because of growing demand and population, its needs are increasing so rapidly that Indonesia may well require all of the world's rice exports by 1985.

The problem, of course, is not simply more food production. Distribution of food also is inadequate and not improving much either. India, whose good harvests are among the most dramatic, currently has enough food to feed its entire population. Poor transportation links to villages, a land reform stalled since partition in 1947, and high rural unemployment have left roughly 30 percent of the 640 million people unable to buy food and hence severely malnourished. Unable to sell to its poor, India has ended up exporting its wheat and rice.

As a result of current low productivity and poor distribution of resources, bad weather in major grain producing countries could cause widespread, outright starvation.

India, again, is a case in point. Between 1975 and 1978, Indian government-held food grain stocks rose from a 10-year low to some 20 million tons. This has reduced the country's short range vulnerability to poor weather and world food shortages—perhaps at some nutritional cost. But India's long-term outlook may not be significantly changed.

Bad weather would quickly wipe out India's reserves.

Current stocks would probably tide the country over one bad monsoon like the 1972 drought. But two bad monsoons similar to those that came back to back in 1965–66 would require all of India's reserves plus an equal amount of imports worth several billion dollars in foreign exchange.

The rest of the world is similarly in jeopardy. Only eleven of the 39 developing countries with food reserve policies have met their targets. Most—including almost all of Asia—have little or no buffer stocks beyond those needed to carry them over to the next harvest. At a recent meeting of Asian and Pacific countries, Arturo Tanco, the Philippine official who heads up the World Food Council, said "One bad crop year could wipe out the ample reserves we have."

The developing world, then, is facing an uncertain future. The developed world—particularly the United States, the granary of the world—must for humanitarian and practical reasons help avert this growing food crisis.

The battle must be fought on three fronts,
  —to raise low agricultural productivity
  —to create food security reserve systems
  —and, to help ensure that food supplies reach the hungry.

At the same time, we must recognize that nothing will succeed unless it centers on the developing countries involved. They must make the programs work. Strategies must fit *their* needs—needs which vary according to supply, production conditions, and consumption requirements, among other things.

As a first step, increasing agricultural productivity is an absolute must. Food production must outdistance population growth, which will remain high in Asia as in other parts of the less developed world.

Fortunately, the prospects for increasing production are good. Most countries in Asia are producing far below reasonable regional rice yield potentials. Agricultural production in Laos, Cambodia, India, the Philippines, Bangladesh, Burma, and Thailand range from less than 20 to 30 percent of the average yields in South Korea and Japan. The International Rice Research Institute in the Philippines has shown that rice production can reach as much as 10 times most current Asian yields.

Helping to bring about higher farm productivity is a dominant theme in the US Agency for International Development's program. Roughly half of our bilateral economic development assistance—approximately 600 million dollars this year—is directed to agricultural and rural development.

Our assistance efforts emphasize a variety of approaches. In Asia we are underwriting agricultural inputs like seeds and fertilizer, supporting irrigation schemes and projects to reduce post-harvest losses, and trying out new marketing techniques that provide incentives to farmers.

A principal program for increasing production encourages use of high yielding varieties of grain, an effort that has already generated important gains. In the mid-1960s, after substantial research in Mexico, high yielding varieties were introduced in the Asian subcontinent. Today, two-thirds of the wheat planted in India and Pakistan is of the high yield variety, and total production has increased to some two and one-half times the 1965 level.

More must be done in this regard. New strains must be developed that flourish without much fertilizer, pesticides or water. Likewise, there is a need for extended research on sustained high-yield cultural practices, including multiple cropping of irrigated areas.

We must also devote greater attention to some of the traditional crops and animals raised by poor farmers on marginal lands and to less widely grown crops that hold promise as new sources of food and income. These will be major agricultural priorities of the Institute for Scientific and Technological Cooperation, a new body which President Carter has proposed and Congress is likely to establish soon.

Current levels of bilateral assistance, however, are not equal to the crisis looming on the horizon. The money crunch that we are feeling in the United States is threatening the foreign aid budget. Consequently, assistance levels this year will at best hold steady in real terms, although expanded financial resources are what we really need.

In addition to higher levels of production, our foreign as-

sistance must seek long range food security. The world needs
a well-stocked larder. For as surely as thunder follows lightning, we can expect that Asia's erratic climate will turn
against the region. The four bumper harvests in South Asia
were made possible to a large extent by unprecedented good
weather. But 40 percent of Asia's rice land is potentially vulnerable to floods—not to mention droughts—and foul
weather is bound to occur again, as it has with grim regularity
throughout history. When it does, yields will decline and im-
porters will bid up food prices.

Sadly we are ill prepared. The concept of government intervention in its agricultural economy to offset the boom and
bust consequences of weather is well established. Virtually
every country tries at least on paper for a rational food policy.
Yet, in the international arena, chaos reigns—with those
countries and peoples at the bottom of the economic ladder
suffering the most.

Regrettably, the International Wheat Council negotiations, which were to establish minimum and maximum indi-
cator prices for wheat as well as buffer stocks to defend them,
floundered recently. The result was an interim agreement to
extend the 1971 agreement for two more years.

This leaves the world with no provision for an interna-
tionally held reserve grain stock to minimize the variability of
world prices and to guard against shortfalls in world production. The failure of the wheat agreement directly affects Japanese and South Asian food security since wheat comprises
nearly 60 percent of their cereal imports, and their total imports account for 30 percent of the wheat sold on international markets.

In a recent speech, Secretary of State Vance indicated
that the United States is preparing to resume wheat negotiations. At the same time, he added that the US—despite the
failure to reach a wheat agreement—would more than double
our minimum 1.9 million ton commitment of food aid. And he
indicated that the government will seek to establish a special
government-held wheat reserve that would add to food security for food-deficit countries.

Other promising approaches for Asia involve individual country and regional food security plans. These schemes have the advantage of meeting the rice-eating needs of the Asian region more directly than a wheat agreement would. Asia-specific food security systems also make sense since the region accounts for 40 percent of the world's present food deficit and because it has common development problems.

ASEAN—the Association of Southeast Asian Nations—has begun to address this food security problem. It has agreed to preferential trade agreements for rice and oil when shortages in the international market occur. ASEAN is also considering a rice stock to be jointly held by member countries.

For its part, the Agency for International Development has begun to consider the utility of combining capital and technical assistance with commodity aid under P.L. 480 programs to help build reserves in LDCs. "Think pieces" prepared for us by the staff of the Food and Feed Grain Institute at Kansas State University indicate that such a program would have enormous benefits for Asian countries.

A recent evaluation of Bangladesh's food supply from 1960–61 through 1976–77 showed, for example, that even with food aid that country did not have one year when food production was in balance with consumption requirements. Each year total supplies were either too high or too low. If AID can help build and manage food storage facilities and lend a hand in filling them, Bangladesh's problem would be alleviated.

As is clear from the foregoing, buffer stocks not only provide for food during times of acute stress. They also create structural improvements in food production by maintaining relatively high and stable price levels.

One concept—called the MOIRA model—has shown that rational international world market price policies, which could be managed by food stockpiles, would also stimulate agricultural production in poor countries. Developed in Europe, the model also shows that if current policies remain unchanged, the world market will have to contend with alternate boom and bust periods. As a result, per capita

consumption in densely populated countries in South Asia
will decline during the period 1975–2010.

As it is today, present surpluses are threatening future
production. Developing countries with surpluses have no
place to store them. They are forced to sell their grain on the
export market where large supplies have depressed prices.
Accordingly governments are getting less for sales than they
paid in subsidies to their farmers to grow the grain. LDC governments can only afford to underwrite these losses for very
short periods of time.

Without a doubt, increases in food production and the
adoption of food reserves policies can play an important role
in alleviating the food/population imbalance in Asia. But
those steps are by themselves not sufficient to completely ease
malnutrition. For even in times of relative plenty as today,
the poor—such as landless laborers in Indonesia who may
earn only a penny or so an hour—go hungry because they
can't afford to buy food.

In this sense the food problem is also an income distribution problem. This recognition has led some to advocate food
transfer approaches not unlike the United States food stamp
program. The major thrust of the international donor community, however, has been toward redirecting the benefits of
growth.

Within AID this "growth with equity" strategy has been
translated into a small farmer strategy designed to alter the
distribution of access to such income producing agricultural
assets as fertilizer, water, and credit. It is not yet clear
whether a strategy based on redistribution of minor assets—
rather than major ones like land—can affect the distribution
of income growth enough to significantly alter the existing
food imbalance. But some of the empirical evidence is not
very comforting. Our harshest critics claim that the technological bias of the high-yielding variety (HYV) production
strategy may actually exacerbate difficulties, although evidence to demonstrate that the absolute income positions of
the poor have deteriorated is sketchy.

Still it is clear that the distribution of the benefits of the
new technology tend to follow existing asset and political

power distributions. In common parlance that means that the rural power structure in poor countries is most likely to benefit first and foremost from new technology, even if we mean to help the poor.

Since most developing countries are characterized by *more* rather than *less* inequality we must worry about the distributional consequences of the new technology. That is, failure to achieve some degree of success in the redistribution of land—land reform—may make it exceedingly difficult to help LDCs overcome malnutrition.

As serious as this is, the distribution of important assets like land is, or course, a touchy political question. Institution of land reform or progressive taxation is generally conceived of as sovereign concern, not as an issue other nations have a right to dictate.

Nevertheless, the need to think about distribution questions remains important. Recognizing this we are pursuing programs like off-farm employment to encourage greater equity and purchasing power. And just as we favor those nations that adopt domestic policies that promote food production, we encourage those LDCs striving for more equitable distribution of resources. At the same time, the US will be participating actively in the upcoming F.A.O. world conference on agrarian reform and rural development that will address this issue.

The long-term payoff of equity-based national actions can be great. Equitable income distribution—like enlightened international price policies—can encourage agricultural production. We have the examples of Taiwan and Korea to show us how equity can spark economic development. Both nations have now graduated from the ranks of US aid recipients and have foreign aid programs of their own.

Thus, real food security in this global village of ours depends on three developments: a better balance between food production and population growth; a food reserve system that guards against disaster; and improved distribution of resources, including food, within and among nations.

If we could even approach the achievement of these objectives, Asia and the world would be set on a course of development that would include not only elimination of starvation and malnutrition, but also furthering of solid programs in the industrial and service sectors as well.

Such developments are in our best interests, too. Helping to build world reserves, for instance, would reduce the burden on the US taxpayer of carrying grain reserves large enough to stabilize world supplies singlehandedly. We could maintain reasonable prices for domestic wheat, rice, and other food grains.

The alternative is to suffer—although to a lesser degree than LDCs—during food shortages. US federal reserve studies have indicated, we should recall, that in 1973–74 rising food prices contributed as much to US and global inflation as did rising oil prices.

Increased reserves, stepped up production, and improved distribution also serve our national security interests. A world racked by hunger, living on the brink of mass starvation is not a stable one.

A better world will not evolve by itself. We, as among the world's rich, must be willing to expend some minor part of our treasure to assist poor nations and poor people. To do so is not only humanitarian, but also insurance against the future.

Like Joseph of the Bible, we must recognize that the fat years need not be only a temporary blessing, but a chance to prepare for the lean years inevitably ahead.

PREVENTION OF THE LAST EPIDEMIC[1]

HOWARD H. HIATT [2]

It is not uncommon to hear careless remarks being made about the possibilities of resorting to atomic warfare to settle interna-

[1] The opening address at the Symposium on the Medical Consequences of Nuclear Weapons and Nuclear War, at 9 A.M., February 9, 1980 in the auditorium of the Harvard University Science Center, Cambridge, Massachusetts.
[2] For biographical note, see Appendix.

tional disputes. The hostage problem in Iran and the Russian invasion of Afghanistan brought a halt to the Salt II talks and gave rise to threats of military retaliation. Some politicians accused President Carter of being timid and vacillating in taking an aggressive stand. In such a climate of international tension, a symposium on the medical consequences of nuclear weapons and nuclear war met February 9 and 10, 1980, under the sponsorship of Physicians for Social Responsibility at the Harvard University Science Center, Cambridge, Massachusetts. The participants included about 600 physicians and concerned citizens.

The opening address was presented by Dr. Howard H. Hiatt of the Harvard School of Public Health at 9 A.M. on February 9. He gave a frightening picture of the cost in human lives and destruction of such warfare and provided convincing evidence of the necessity for "the progressive removal of nuclear weapons" from the arena of international conflict. The power in his speech can be found in his skillfull development of analogies between past epidemics and nuclear "epidemics." Citing the results of the 1945 atomic bomb attack on Japan, he describes the likely consequences of a hypothetical attack on Boston. His excellent use of support facts gives unusual urgency to his arguments for preventing the ultimate, nuclear epidemic.

In a ten-day period in 1854 an epidemic of cholera resulted in over 500 deaths in the Golden Square area of London. Although the cause of the disease was then unknown, an English physician, John Snow, suspected from the patterns of previous attacks that it was transmitted by sewage-contaminated water. At that time, each London district had its own water supply, and the distribution of cases led Snow to suspect a pump on Broad Street as the source of contaminated water. When the pump handle was removed, the epidemic ended—a triumph of public health practice.

Our definition of the word "epidemic" has broadened since those days. For example, the 100,000 Americans that will die this year of cancer of the lung must be considered as victims of a new kind of epidemic. The number of deaths from lung cancer among American males has increased more than 15-fold in the past 50 years. The outlook for the patient with lung cancer has not changed perceptibly—fewer than 10 percent of those people who contract the disease will be cured. Simultaneously, costs of health services have risen steeply; this year they will exceed $200 billion.

A growing awareness of the limitations of many therapeutic measures and their mounting costs have led to increased attention to preventive approaches to major health problems. High on that list is lung cancer, particularly because of its clear-cut relationship to cigarette smoking. It is widely recognized, however, that demonstration of the cause of a disease does not guarantee its control. In the instance of cigarette smoking and lung cancer, for example, multiple approaches are being made and experts have been enlisted from many disciplines—medicine, economics, law, behavioral science, chemistry, political science, and government, as well as all concerned citizens. Although the progress that has been made to date to control the lung cancer epidemic has been admittedly modest, the attention given the problem has surely had some beneficial effects.

In the two days ahead, we shall consider yet another kind of epidemic, or more accurately a group of epidemics. Here the term epidemic is stretched beyond any meaning previously known. I refer, of course, to the epidemic that would result from the use of nuclear weapons. The speakers that follow will discuss aspects of these epidemics—their causes in physical and political terms; their modes of expression—short, intermediate and long term; and the prospects for their control. The magnitude of death, suffering, destruction, and desolation that would result from the smallest conceivable nuclear war and the ineffectiveness of available medical interventions permit only one approach to the problem—that of prevention. The only route to prevention, in turn, is progressive removal of nuclear weapons.

A major reason for this symposium on the medical consequences of nuclear war is the relative neglect of this topic in our national and international dialogue. In contrast to widespread belief, much can be said about the catastrophe that would follow the use of nuclear weapons. Much can also be said about the limitations of existing methods of medical intervention. Perhaps so little is said about the catastrophe because it is horrible to contemplate. Surely, so little is said about intervention because so little that is hopeful can be said. And yet, by our very silence we risk permitting or encouraging the nuclear arms race to continue. This, in turn, makes almost inevitable, either by design or by chance, what could be the last epidemic our civilization will know.

The Clinical Picture

What are some immediate effects that would follow the use of a nuclear weapon? Dr. Lifton, who will speak later today, on his book, *Death in Life: Survivors of Hiroshima*, offers the following description:

The bomb was completely on target and exploded, with a force equivalent to twenty thousand pounds of TNT, eighteen hundred feet in the air near the center of a flat city built mainly of wood. It created an area of total destruction (including residential, commercial, industrial, and military structures) extending three thousand meters . . . in all directions; and destroyed sixty thousand of ninety thousand buildings within five thousand meters . . . an area roughly encompassing the city limits. Flash burns from the heat generated by the release of an enormous amount of radiant energy occurred at distances of more than four thousand meters . . . depending upon the type and amount of clothing worn and the shielding afforded by immediate surroundings. Injuries from the blast and from splintered glass and falling debris, occurred throughout the city and beyond.

Soon after the bomb fell—sometimes within hours or even minutes, often during the first twenty-four hours or the following days and weeks—survivors began to notice in themselves and others a strange form of illness. It consisted of nausea, vomiting, and loss of appetite; diarrhea with large amounts of blood in the stools; fever and weakness; purple spots on various parts of the body from bleeding into the skin . . . ; inflammation and ulceration of the mouth, throat, and gums . . . ; bleeding from the mouth, gums, throat, rectum, and urinary tract . . . ; loss of hair from the scalp and other parts of the body . . . extremely low white blood cell counts . . . and in many cases a progressive course until death. The gastrointestinal symptoms appeared first and the hemorrhagic manifestations and other bone marrow effects some weeks later, so that the overall syndrome only gradually revealed itself.

Overall casualties in this city of 245,000 are not accurately documented. It is estimated that 100,000 died in the bombing, about 25 percent directly burned by the bomb, 50 percent from other injuries, and 20 percent as a result of radiation effects. As horrifying as are the statistics, perhaps even more devastating are the descriptions of individual victims. Consider this picture presented by John Hersey in his book, *Hiroshima:*

> When he had penetrated the bushes, he saw there were about 20 men, and they were all in exactly the same nightmarish state: their faces were wholly burned, their eye sockets were hollow, the fluid from their melted eyes had run down their cheeks. (They must have had their faces upturned when the bomb went off; perhaps they were anti-aircraft personnel.) Their mouths were mere swollen, pus-covered wounds, which they could not bear to stretch enough to admit the spout of the teapot. So Father Kleinsorge got a large piece of grass and drew out the stem so as to make a straw and gave them all water to drink that way.

The picture of the devastation wrought by an atomic weapon in Hiroshima represents, along with the similar experience in Nagasaki, first-hand knowledge of the consequences of nuclear warfare, but there are many theoretical appraisals upon which we may also draw.

Since that traumatic beginning of the nuclear age, scientists, military theoreticians, and national security planners have attempted to project the Hiroshima-Nagasaki data forward in order to understand the human and material consequences of a nuclear attack upon an American city. One such study, prepared by the Joint Congressional Committee on Atomic Energy in 1959, postulated a 1,446-megaton attack on a number of American cities, including Boston. Three years later, a series of articles in the *New England Journal of Medicine* gave further consideration to the hypothetical attack on Boston, itself, and that is the source upon which I have drawn for these remarks. Dr. Mark will consider in detail the implications of a nuclear attack on Boston. For the brief remarks that follow, bear in mind that the assumptions of this two-decade old study are now quite conservative.

While the 20 megaton weapon involved in this hypothetical attack is far more destructive than the Hiroshima and Nagasaki bombs (10 and 20 kilotons, respectively), so, too, is it far less destructive than the largest contemporary weapons. And as horrifying as the postulated effects of this attack are on the local population, the numbers used in preparing the analysis were drawn from the 1950 census.

Boston's trial by nuclear attack begins with the detonation of a 20 megaton bomb exploding at ground level in the city's downtown area. The explosion excavates a massive crater, half a mile in diameter and several hundred feet deep, but the area of total destruction, the circle within which even the most heavily reinforced concrete structures do not survive, has a radius of four miles. From the ocean to Watertown; from Everett to Dorchester, the destruction is complete. This circle includes within it most of the hospitals, clinics, and medical personnel in the Boston area.

At a distance of six miles from the center of the blast, an area including Newton, Melrose, Arlington and Milton, all frame or brick buildings, are badly damaged, but not destroyed.

As far away as Saugus, Natick, Quincy, Weston and Lexington, 15 miles from the blast, all frame buildings are damaged beyond repair Such is the immediate damage resulting from the bomb's blast effects, alone. But the detonation of the bomb also released a tremendous amount of thermal energy.

More than 20 miles from the blast people suffer second-degree burns on all exposed skin and additional burns from flammable clothing and environmental materials. As far as 40 miles away, retinal burns resulting from looking at the fireball causes blindness. The pressure wave released by the bomb travels outward from the center at greater than the speed of sound. That wave is followed by winds which exceed 1,000 miles per hour fanning the many fires caused by the initial blast and thermal radiation.

As far from the hypocenter as 21 miles, the growing fire storm is fueled by igniting houses, foliage, and oil and gasoline storage tanks. As in Dresden and Hamburg, the fire storm alone accounts for many deaths and injuries and increases the already catastrophic physical damage caused by the blast.

Within the four mile radius of complete destruction, more than 739,000 persons lie dead. Within the radius of the fire storm, an additional 1.5 million deaths occur. There are thus more than 2.2 million fatalities in the metropolitan area caused by blast and fire storms alone. Many of the survivors are badly burned, blinded, and otherwise seriously wounded. Many are disoriented. These are the short-term effects; the problem of radiation sickness will grow in the days and weeks ahead.

The population is devastated; many of the survivors are in need of immediate medical care, food, shelter, clothing, and water. The cities in which they lived have, in many cases, virtually ceased to exist as physical entities—and as social entities as well.

Government is barely existent. The transportation system and many roads have been destroyed. Remaining food, water, and medical supplies are dangerously inadequate. The physicians and other professionals needed to treat the survivors and reestablish administrative mechanisms for coping with the crisis are as decimated as the population as a whole. That is the clinical picture of a major American city and its metropolitan area under the conditions of a hypothetical nuclear disaster.

The Medical Response

I referred earlier to a growing awareness of the limitations of therapeutic medicine as one important reason for the increased interest in prevention. I spoke of the shortcomings of treatment programs for lung cancer. How would modern medicine deal with the casualties of a nuclear attack? John Hersey describes the problems presented to Hiroshima's medical care system and its capabilities and response:

Of a hundred and fifty doctors in the city, sixty-five were already dead and most of the rest were wounded. Of 1,780 nurses, 1,654 were dead or too badly hurt to work. In the biggest hospital, that of the Red Cross, only six doctors out of thirty were able to function, and only 10 nurses out of more than two hundred . . . At least 10,000 of the (city's) wounded made their way to the (Red Cross Hospital) which was altogether unequal to such a trampling, since it had only 600 beds, and they had all been occupied.

Again, examining the problems in terms of individuals, Hersey presents an even grimmer picture:

Dr. Sasaki worked without method, taking those who were nearest to him first, and he noticed soon that the corridor seemed to be getting more and more crowded. Mixed in with the abrasions and lacerations which most people in the hospital had suffered, he began to find dreadful burns. He realized then that casualties were pouring in from outdoors. There were so many that he began to pass up the lightly wounded; he decided that all he could hope to do was to stop people from bleeding to death. Before long, patients lay and crouched on the floors of the wards and the laboratories and all other rooms, and in the corridors, and on the stairs, and in the front hall, and under the porte cochere, and on the stone front steps, and in the driveway and courtyard, and for blocks each way in the streets outside. Wounded peole supported maimed people; disfigured families leaned together. Many people were vomiting. A tremendous number of school-girls—some of those who had been taken from their classrooms to work outdoors, clearing fire lanes—crept into the hospital. The people in the suffocating crowd inside the hospital wept and cried, for Dr. Sasaki to hear, "Sensei! Doctor." and the less seriously wounded came and pulled at his sleeve and begged him to go to the aid of the worse wounded. Tugged here and there in his stocking feet, bewildered by the numbers, staggered by so much raw flesh, Dr. Sasaki lost all sense of profession and stopped working as a skillful surgeon and a sympathetic man; he became an automaton, mechanically wiping, daubing, winding, wiping, daubing, winding.

We considered the dimensions of the catastrophe that Boston and its citizens would experience in the event of a nuclear attack. In the aftermath of such a disaster, problems of treatment and management become paramount. But what resources would be available to attack those problems?

Using as their base a figure of 6,560 physicians in the Boston metropolitan area at the time of attack, the 1959 and 1962 studies project that almost 5,000 would be killed immediately or fatally injured, and that only 900 would be in condition to render post-attack medical care. The ratio of injured persons to physicians would thus be in excess of 1,700 to one.

If a physician spent an average of only 15 minutes with each injured person and worked sixteen hours each day, the studies project, it would take from 16 to 26 days for each casualty to be seen once. And even this estimate, the *New England Journal* study admitted "is unreasonably optimistic."

The number of hospital beds would have been reduced by at least five-sixths and the amount of medical equipment and supplies would be similarly inadequate. The geographic distribution of such resources in the post-attack period would be another problem, perhaps requiring physicians to enter more highly radioactive areas, and thus expose themselves to greater personal danger, in order to treat the injured.

Physicians will be faced with large numbers of patients with blast injuries, including lacerations of soft tissues and fractures; thermal injuries, including surface burns, retinal burns, and respiratory-tract damage; and radiation injuries, including acute radiation syndrome and delayed effects. Infectious diseases will be rampant because of lower resistance and widespread contamination. Severe psychological problems will be widespread.

"The medical problems of the post-attack period," according to the *New England Journal* study, "will require more of a public-health orientation than many practicing physicians will hitherto utilize. In a society struggling for survival adequate sanitation and the provision of food and water may save more lives than the most skilled specialist care ... the control of epidemic disease will constitute an ever present challenge."

Among one of the most serious of the post-attack public health problems, although among the least frequently discussed, is disposal of the dead. The presence of more than 2.2 million dead bodies in the metropolitan area will pose a continuing and serious hazard to the health of the survivors.

The overwhelming problems confronting professionals in

nuclear-devastated Boston are the medical care of, and restoration of essential services to, a population with greatly increased needs. A drastically reduced number of professionals might stand a chance of providing some help if the physical infrastructure of the area remained essentially undamaged. If, on the other hand, most of the professionals were to survive the attack, they might be able to discharge some of their responsibilities, even in the face of a seriously damaged infrastructure. Under the more realistic projections of a decimated professional community and an all but destroyed infrastructure, however, the problems of treatment and management become overwhelming.

Note that I leave to the more detailed presentations that follow a consideration of the equally dreadful intermediate and long-term effects of the nuclear attack on the surviving population.

Magnitude of the Problem

At present more than 50,000 nuclear warheads are deployed and ready. Most dwarf in destructive power the bomb used against Hiroshima. Sufficient nuclear bombs exist outside the United States to subject every major American city repeatedly to the destruction that was described for Boston. Six nations are now acknowledged possessors of nuclear weapons, but other countries almost surely share that "privilege." Every addition to this list increases the degree of instability.

Conclusions

The preparation of these remarks was for me a stressful experience. What purpose, I wondered initially, to describe such almost unthinkable conditions. But the conditions are not unthinkable; rather they are infrequently thought about. As Professor Victor Weisskopf points out in the current *Bulletin of the Atomic Scientists*, it is "surprising and most depressing that the public and most of the interested scientists rarely discuss . . . the dangers of nuclear war." Among the painful results of the silence are the continuing proliferation of nuclear weapons and the failure to reject out-of-hand nuclear war as a "viable option" in the management of world problems. Indeed, incredible as it may seem to any reasonable person, we hear with increasing frequency proposals that we consider launching limited nuclear attacks and even suggestions that we might "win" a nuclear war.

We have come together to break the silence on the issue. An objective examination of the certain medical consequences of a nuclear war and the probable medical consequences of failure to limit severely nuclear weapons leads to but one conclusion: prevention is our only recourse. There is, in fact, no reason to consider the consequences of nuclear war in strictly medical terms. But if we do so, we must pay heed to the inescapable lesson of contemporary medicine: where treatment of a given disease is ineffective *or* where costs are insupportable, attention must be given to prevention. Both conditions apply to the effects of nuclear war—treatment programs would be virtually useless and the costs would be staggering. Can any stronger arguments be marshalled for a preventive strategy?

Prevention of this final epidemic will be more difficult than removing the handle of the Broad Street pump and more difficult than the control of cigarette smoking.

On logical grounds one might expect it to be simpler. After all, the association of the cholera epidemic with contaminated water and of the lung cancer epidemic with cigarettes were epidemiologic triumphs. In contrast, no special skills are required to associate the clinical picture of Hiroshima with the single object dropped from the sky by the Enola Gay on August 6, 1945. Further, treatment for the victims of nuclear weapons is far more futile than that for cholera in 1854 and that for lung cancer in 1980, and surely no effective therapeutic measures are on the horizon. Prevention, then, is critical, and nobody is more qualified to disseminate that message than physicians. But, as I pointed out with respect to lung cancer, preventive medicine must be the province of experts from many disciplines and, indeed, of everybody. Clearly, this reality applies far more forcefully to prevention of nuclear war.

We believe that the discussions of these two days will lead to the following conclusions. First, the rewards for making the effort and succeeding in preventing this epidemic will be far richer than the control of cholera, lung cancer, or any other disease known to man. Second, the cost of making the effort and failing will be horror beyond description. Finally, the cost of *not* making the effort will include as well, an insupportable betrayal of ourselves and of our children.

"IF WE FALL DOWN IN THE LAND OF PEACE"[1]

Mark O. Hatfield[2]

Senator Mark O. Hatfield (Republican, Oregon) delivered a lay sermon at the Sunday morning service of the San Antonio, Texas, First Baptist Church at 11:00 A.M. on September 30, 1979 before a congregation of about 2,000 members as well as a television audience. As a devoted Christian, the Oregon Senator speaks frequently to church groups and at worship services. Drawing his text from Jeremiah 12, he applied his Christian convictions to world issues, giving what he called a message of "hope," not of "despair." In contemplating the world today, the Senator exhorted his congregation to act, to conserve, and not to be "fearful to stand against the wind." The speech reveals that he has a grasp of homiletics.

It is interesting how he developed his speech. In a letter to this editor (April 22, 1980) Hatfield wrote:

—Actually, I was prepared to speak that morning on another topic, "Healing Love" when in conversation with the Pastor, Dr. Jimmy Allen, it became apparent that they wanted something more focused on world issues. So in the 20 minutes between when the service started and the appointed moment for me to speak, I jot-

---

[1] Delivered at the morning service, First Baptist Church, San Antonio, Texas, September 30, 1979. Quoted by permission.
[2] For biographical note, see Appendix.

ted down a few thoughts and built it upon the Jeremiah
12 passage. I since have used it several times in Sunday
morning church services but the essential outline has remained unchanged since that service in Texas.

Hatfield, a former college professor, is one senator who does
not hesitate to speak frankly about the preparation of his speeches.
Answering an inquiry about his *inventio* in another letter, he said,

As you would expect, my staff provides assistance
with the research and drafting of many of my speeches.
In formal situations for which there must be prepared
remarks, I generally use rather complete outlines. Many
times I depart from these in the delivery and sometimes
set them aside altogether to use different material. Thus
it could not be accurately said that my staff "writes" my
speeches, for I am actively involved in the process. They
consult me initially on the topic and submit rough drafts
to me for review and correction. This interaction helps
the staff to anticipate my preferences on style and substance when working on material for other speeches.
(letter to John W. Kelton, October 30, 1978)

During the past decade, three other Hatfield speeches have
appeared in *Representative American Speeches* (see 1972–73;
1973–74; and 1974–75).

If you have run with footmen and they have tired you out, then
how can you compete with the horses? If you fall down in the land
of peace, how will you do in the thicket of the Jordan?

These words from the ancient prophet, Jeremiah, perhaps
more eloquently than any I know speak to us today. As we
think of the world in which we live, the attitudes, the problems, the issues [that] the people sense and [that they] realize
confront us all, these prophetic words ring true. Because of
your global awareness theme, I have chosen the challenge of
Jeremiah.

We are fully aware that there are many parallelisms that
exist. Let me repeat those words from the Living Bible:

How long must this land of yours put up with all their goings
on? Even the grass of the field groans and weeps over their wicked
deeds. The wild animals and birds have moved away, leaving the

land deserted. Yet the people say, "God won't judge on us. We are perfectly safe." If racing with mere men and these men of Anathoth has wearied you, how will you race against horses, against the king, his court, and all his evil priests? If you stumble and fall on open ground, what will you do in Jordan's jungle? . . . Destroying armies plunder the land. The sword of the Lord devours from one end of the nation to the other. Nothing shall escape. My people have sown wheat but reaped thorns. They have worked hard but it does them no good. They shall harvest a crop of shame, for the fierce anger of the Lord is upon them. . . . And if these heathen nations quickly learn my people's ways and claim me as their God instead of Baal, then they shall be strong among my people. [Jeremiah 12:4-16]

Let me suggest three particular views of the world today.

There are those who see the world as an explosion of difficulties created through remarkable and geometric expansion of growth. It has required the earth two million years to reach our first one billion people. In fact, at the beginning of the Christian era two thousand years ago, there were only an estimated 250 million people on the earth. By 1830 the earth had grown to a billion people. Only one hundred years later, in 1930, the world had reached two billion people. Then in only thirty years, in 1960, it had reached three billion people. And only 16 years later, in 1976, it had reached four billion people. In but 14 more years, in 1990, it will reach five billion people. Only 10 years from then, in the year 2000, it will have reached six billion people.

This indeed is the world in which we live. Each person born into this world will demand certain requirements to have life sustained. As the world gets larger through this explosion of population, the pie gets smaller. We have difficulty today in dividing the pie. What will it be when it is one billion people more, two billion more and three billion more?

There are those who look upon the world in a second way. They see the world as a finite globe, limited by its resources with the growing population placing a heavier demand upon those diminishing resources.

We know that it takes 13 basic raw materials and minerals to sustain the super industrial machine of the United States of America. We had to import over 50 percent of only one of those—one of the 13—in 1900. In 1950, the number had increased to three of the 13 that we had to import to supply over 50 percent of our need. In 1960, it grew to six. In 1980, it will grow to nine. By the year 2000, the United States of America will have to import 12 of the 13 basic raw materials to sustain our economic life.

We have experienced this in the petroleum field. But it will expand more rapidly into other fields that are perhaps less noticeable in the direct consumption pattern but, nevertheless, vital raw materials that we need.

So the voice is heard. If we fall down in a land of peace, what will we do in the thicket of the Jordan as this world changes?

Thirdly, there are those who see the world as a vast military arsenal. The competition between various ideologies is responded to by escalation of greater and more deadly weapons.

I walked in the streets of Hiroshima as a naval officer a few weeks after the bomb had been dropped in World War II. All the bodies had not yet been pulled out of the rubble to be buried; you smelled them, you saw them; and I experienced this vast devastation, created by one bomb. The ambivalence was intense that I had, knowing the bomb probably saved my life and many hundreds of thousands of other people's lives—we were staging for the invasion of Japan at the time the bomb was dropped—and yet knowing one bomb had wracked this kind of devastation upon one city.

My friends, today our arsenal in this nation is the equivalent of 625,000 Hiroshima bombs. Myths are perpetrated in this nation today about arms limitation . . . we doubled our warheads under SALT I, we'll increase them under SALT II, and by the time, if we ever get and I doubt we ever will get to SALT III, we'll have the equivalency of two million Hiroshima bombs and the Soviet Union will have the equivalency of two million Hiroshima bombs.

The more we build, the less security we have in hardware. The Shah of Iran was crushed by his military hardware, because he neglected the social, the economic, the political, the spiritual deficiencies and problems of his nation.

If you fall down in a land of peace, what will you do in the thicket of the Jordan? What will we do with all that kill power? Does it bring us security? Does it bring us greater power? Does it bring us greater prestige? So there are, then, today these various perspectives of the world—the world that is exploiting people, the world that is diminishing in resources, the world that is increasing in its capacity to destroy itself. What are our reactions? What are the responses? What does the Christian have to say to this world, especially at a "global view conference?"

Immediately these things will repel some people. They will throw up their hands and say, "Come, Lord, come quickly. The only way out is for the Second Advent." We all pray for the Lord's return, of course. But until the Lord is back with us in His great Second Coming, what are we about? We should be about the Father's business.

There will be those who will say, "let us isolate ourselves," and withdraw from the world. It reminds me of my research on the bill that I introduced in the United States Senate two years ago to restore the citizenship of the President of the Confederacy, Jefferson Davis. I came to appreciate in a new way the greatness of this American. I ran across a letter that he had written long after the war between the states. In 1888, he wrote, in his letter to Mrs. Woodbury: "We are living far from the world, not forgetting, though we may be forgot, save by such kind hearts as yours, which are drawn to friends by their misfortunes rather than repelled by them."

Isn't that a beautiful expression? Do not be repelled by these great problems, but in effect we as Christians should be drawn to them. We should be drawn because we recognize that we are the open door to the agony and to the pain and to the hurt and to the questions and to the doubts, to the confusion, to the fears that people have about the world in which we live. We are the open door and if we are not, we are not fulfilling that which God has called us to perform.

I know it's so easy to ignore or to hide or to withdraw. This was eloquently demonstrated by the memoirs of Pastor Niemoller during the rise of Hitler's regime in Germany. In reflecting upon that particular period of time, Pastor Nie-

moller, who was a pastor of the great confessing church of
Germany, said how easy it was to ignore even those circumstances that were so immediately about you. He said, "first,
the Nazis came for the Communists. And I did not speak up,
for I was not a Communist. And then the Nazis came for the
Jews and I did not speak up for I was not a Jew. Then the
Nazis came for the trade unionists and I did not speak up, for
I was not a trade unionist. And then the Nazis came for the
Catholics and I did not speak up for I was a Protestant. And
then, finally, the Nazis came for me and by this time, there
was no one left to speak up for anyone."

It's so easy, so much easier to get along by going along;
yet, Christ calls us to be a subculture. Christ calls us to with-
stand the values and the standards that are set by culture and
the world. So frequently we do not hear, we do not listen. We
are fearful to stand against the wind. We are fearful to stand
alone, even when we know it's right. And yet how often we
see in Paul's life and his journeys he stood alone, even when
some of his friends and his fellow churchmen faded away.

We are called to action. We are called to be involved in
this world. It may not be much . . . I may have little talent,
but whatever it is, if it's committed to Jesus Christ, he will use
it. Bob Pierce (the founder of World Vision) once said: "I
can't do everything for everyone, but I can do something for
someone."

Mother Teresa, in Calcutta, has been called by God to
minister to the dying on the streets of Calcutta. When I had
the privilege of spending a day with her, I looked at the magnitude of the problem and was struck with a sense of hope-
lessness when I looked at the logistics and the statistics. She
said, "we pick them up, day by day, those who are dying. We
wash them and we clean them. We try to feed them and we
tell them about Jesus before they die."

How many will be in heaven because of the commitment
of one person who didn't look at the impossibility and the
magnitude of the global problems, but on a one-to-one basis,
began to do something about it.

In 391 there was an Eastern Monk by the name of Telemachus who came from his monastary to Rome for the first

time and was appalled at the gladiatorial circuses of people killing one another for the bloody enjoyment of the audience. He was so moved by the Holy Spirit, he jumped down into the arena. He went to those who were the gladiatorial combatants and he said, "Stop, in the name of Christ!" They were so stunned and overwhelmed by the courage of one man, they put down their weapons. The crowd became so frenzied that they came into the arena and literally tore the limbs from the body of Telemachus. But Emperor Heronius heard about the courage of this one man. He was so compelled by God's Spirit that he issued a fiat and abolished the gladiatorial circuses. One involved man's courage made the difference.

Secondly, how do we respond to the resources and their diminishing situation as we confront them? We go back to the Scripture. God created all things for man's use. "Subdue the earth. Utilize it wisely."

But you see, He told us that we own nothing. This is one of our hang-ups today. We play games with one another. We have titles and deeds as if we own something and we possess it entirely, exclusively, outside of God's creation. We believe in God as the Creator; we cannot divest the Creator of His creation. But we are called to be stewards. We own nothing. We are stewards over that which he has given to us for wise utilization.

We are bowing down before Baal today in this country and Baal is manifest in convenience and disposability. We want products in the marketplace that are going to bring us convenience and disposability. And we are paying the price—a price of squander, exploitation, and waste while others are starving.

Look at the changes that have been made since World War II. We used to have fibers that were grown by free solar energy—wool and cotton, now displaced by synthetics that place a heavy demand upon energy. We used to have building materials that came out of the forests, grown by free solar energy, now replaced by plastics and glass and mortar and all the other things that place a heavy demand upon energy and have a debilitating impact upon our environment.

We must restore the Christian concept of stewardship.

That's what the Christian has to say to the world today. We will conserve. We will use wisely. We will not exploit in a consumer oriented economy that says, "use it, throw it away." The throw away ethic has to be replaced by the conservation ethic.

Lastly, what do we say about the military machine? In 1945, in Alamogordo, New Mexico, as that first atomic weapon was detonated, there was a noise and a rush of wind and one of the observers said it seemed almost blasphemous that we had unleashed power that heretofore had been reserved only for the Almighty. The death of one is a tragedy. But the death of a million is a statistic. We handle that today in our Pentagon and all over the world, in all governments, in the same computerized manner so that we can tolerate the loss of ten million, or 100 million people in a war.

But let us remember this . . . the true power of the nation is its spiritual power. We must learn that, not only by the facts of history, but by the demands of today. We can have all the hardware and all the bombs in the world and it will not save us. If this nation is weak from inside, then the Christian has this to say to the militarious mind of today: Power is in the Lord God Almighty. It is in that power I put my trust and my hope and my security.

I am not suggesting that we have reached that millenia, turning our swords into ploughshares. What I am saying is we have lost the balance and we are denying people the basic needs of life.

It was a great military leader himself, Dwight Eisenhower, who said "a time will come where every dollar that you spend for a rocket, for a gun, for a cannon, for a plane, becomes a theft, an actual theft, from the people who are hungry and do not have food; people who are not housed and people who are not clothed." And he said, "that will not make the nation stronger, that will make the nation weaker." This came from a five star general, not from Jeremiah. How are we doing in the thicket today, we might ask ourselves?

John Adams observed that the American Revolution was not the war of 1776. He said that had nothing to do with the

Revolution. It was the consequence of the Revolution. For, John Adams said, the true American Revolution was in the hearts and the minds of the citizens when they covenanted one with another to a new set of values, new principles. They were willing to live and die for them. That was the American Revolution.

That's what I would call for today to answer those who say our power and our security are found only in our gold or our guns. That security is false doctrine and the Christian must speak up and not let the nation be lured off into such pathways. The security of this nation will ultimately and only be determined by the spirituality. Are we committed to God, living His life, ministering to His people?

This is not a message of despair, this is a message of hope. We have looked at the world and only through three perspectives this morning. But, my dear friends, we are gathered in God's house, not to bemoan the facts and circumstances in which we find ourselves, because ours is a God of faith and not a God of circumstances! Thereby we have that unlimited power of God himself because again, as in the case of that very interesting period of Jeremiah, let me repeat:

And if these heathen nations quickly learn my people's ways and claim me as their God instead of Baal, they shall be strong among our people.

I suggest to you today that as we can sing together, Hosanna, Jesus Christ is the King of Kings, we have not only the person and the source of our true security, we have the lessons one by one of how we can respond to the world in a powerful believing community moved by the Holy Spirit: to minister to those people, however many there may be; to proclaim the good news of salvation; to meet their physical needs as well as their spiritual needs; to reassure them that God is a God of history; and, that all the woes of the day should not bear us down to the point where we stumble in a land of peace. We march against the chariots and we stand in the land of peace and we will not stumble in the thicket of the Jordan.

NATIONAL PRIORITIES

ENERGY AND THE NATIONAL GOALS[1]

JIMMY CARTER [2]

During the year President Jimmy Carter has faced a long, hard road, as he moved from one crisis to another: energy, inflation, hostages in Iran, and the Russian invasion of Afghanistan. In dealing with each crisis, the President presented his position via radio and television. Any one of these statements deserves a place in this volume as representative of his rhetoric. However, the speech that received the most favorable comment and seemed to check the downward plunge of his popularity was his address on July 15, 1979, when he presented his proposals to alleviate the energy crisis.

The President originally planned to speak on energy on July 5, but cancelled that appearance in order to gain more background about the crisis. This move increased public anticipation of what his position would be on so vital a subject.

Between July 6 and 11, at Camp David, the President conferred with one hundred and thirty-five persons, including governors, congressmen, journalists, businessmen, labor leaders, black leaders, educators, economists, religious leaders, and mayors (for list see *Newsweek*, Jl. 23, '79, p 25). After hours of conference and much advice, President Carter felt ready to speak. Frank Reynolds of ABC declared that the speech was "the most eagerly awaited one of the Carter Administration."

The title of the speech indicates the bifurcated nature of his presentation. After reciting, verbatim, bits of advice he had received from those he had consulted, and analyzing the mood of the American people, he proposed six actions that would not only solve the energy crisis, but restore the American spirit. The thirty-three minute speech was delivered from the Oval Office at the White House at 10 P.M. (EST) and was carried live on radio and television to an estimated viewing public of 60 million people (NY *Times*, Jl. 17, '79). Eighty million listeners had slipped in recent months to 30 million. The consensus of reporters and other observ-

---

[1] Delivered from the Oval Office, White House, Washington, D.C., at 10 P.M. (EST), July 15, 1979 via radio and television.
[2] For biographical note, see Appendix.

ers was that he was more effective on this occasion than he had been previously; several agreed with Frank Reynolds of ABC that the speech was "almost a sermon." A Christian Science *Monitor* editorial called it "eloquent and forthright" (Jl. 17, '79), and the St. Louis *Post Dispatch*, his "best venture" (quoted in NY *Times*, Jl. 17, '79, p A13).

Good evening.

This is a special night for me. Exactly three years ago, on July 15, 1976, I accepted the nomination of my party to run for President of the United States. I promised you a President who is not isolated from the people, who feels your pain, and who shares your dreams and who draws his strength and his wisdom from you.

During the past three years I've spoken to you on many occasions about national concerns, the energy crisis, reorganizing the government, our nation's economy, and issues of war and especially peace. But over those years the subjects of the speeches, the talks, and the press conferences have become increasingly narrow, focused more and more on what the isolated world of Washington thinks is important. Gradually, you've heard more and more about what the government thinks or what the government should be doing and less and less about our nation's hopes, our dreams, and our vision of the future.

Ten days ago I had planned to speak to you again about a very important subject—energy. For the fifth time I would have described the urgency of the problem and laid out a series of legislative recommendations to the Congress. But as I was preparing to speak, I began to ask myself the same question that I now know has been troubling many of you. Why have we not been able to get together as a nation to resolve our serious energy problem?

It's clear that the true problems of our nation are much deeper—deeper than gasoline lines or energy shortages, deeper even than inflation or recession. And I realize more than ever that as President I need your help. So, I decided to reach out and listen to the voices of America.

I invited to Camp David people from almost every segment of our society—business and labor, teachers and preachers, governors, mayors, and private citizens. And then I left Camp David to listen to other Americans, men and women like you. It has been an extraordinary ten days, and I want to share with you what I've heard.

First of all, I got a lot of personal advice. Let me quote a few of the typical comments that I wrote down.

This from a southern governor: "Mr. President, you are not leading this nation—you're just managing the government."

"You don't see the people enough any more."

"Some of your Cabinet members don't seem loyal. There is not enough discipline among your disciples."

"Don't talk to us about politics or the mechanics of government, but about an understanding of our common good."

"Mr. President, we're in trouble. Talk to us about blood and sweat and tears."

"If you lead, Mr. President, we will follow."

Many people talked about themselves and about the condition of our nation. This from a young woman in Pennsylvania:

"I feel so far from government. I feel like ordinary people are excluded from political power."

And this from a young Chicano:

"Some of us have suffered from recession all our lives."

"Some people have wasted energy, but others haven't had anything to waste."

And this from a religious leader:

"No material shortage can touch the important things like God's love for us or our love for one another."

And I like this one particularly from a black woman who happens to be the mayor of a small Mississippi town:

"The big-shots are not the only ones who are important. Remember, you can't sell anything on Wall Street unless someone digs it up somewhere else first."

This kind of summarized a lot of other statements:

"Mr. President, we are confronted with a moral and a spiritual crisis."

Several of our discussions were on energy, and I have a notebook full of comments and advice. I'll read just a few.

"We can't go on consuming 40 percent more energy than we produce. When we import oil we are also importing inflation plus unemployment."

"We've got to use what we have. The Middle East has only 5 percent of the world's energy, but the United States has 24 percent."

And this is one of the most vivid statements:

"Our neck is stretched over the fence and OPEC has a knife."

"There will be other cartels and other shortages. American wisdom and courage right now can set a path to follow in the future."

This was a good one:

"Be bold, Mr. President. We may make mistakes, but we are ready to experiment."

And this one from a labor leader got to the heart of it:

"The real issue is freedom. We must deal with the energy problem on a war footing."

And the last that I'll read:

"When we enter the moral equivalent of war, Mr. President, don't issue us BB guns."

These ten days confirmed my belief in the decency and the strength and the wisdom of the American people, but it also bore out some of my longstanding concerns about our nation's underlying problems.

I know, of course, being President, that government actions and legislation can be very important. That's why I've worked hard to put my campaign promises into law—and I have to admit, with just mixed success. But after listening to the American people I have been reminded again that all the legislation in the world can't fix what's wrong with America. So, I want to speak to you first tonight about a subject even more serious than energy or inflation. I want to talk to you right now about a fundamental threat to American democracy.

I do not mean our political and civil liberties. They will endure. And I do not refer to the outward strength of America, a nation that is at peace tonight everywhere in the world, with unmatched economic power and military might.

The threat is nearly invisible in ordinary ways. It is a crisis of confidence. It is a crisis that strikes at the very heart and soul and spirit of our national will. We can see this crisis in the growing doubt about the meaning of our own lives and in the loss of a unity of purpose for our nation.

The erosion of our confidence in the future is threatening to destroy the social and the political fabric of America.

The confidence that we have always had as a people is not simply some romantic dream or a proverb in a dusty book that we read just on the Fourth of July. It is the idea which founded our nation and has guided our development as a people. Confidence in the future has supported everything else—public institutions and private enterprise, our own families, and the very Constitution of the United States. Confidence has defined our course and has served as a link between generations. We've always believed in something called progress. We've always had a faith that the days of our children would be better than our own.

Our people are losing that faith, not only in government itself but in the ability as citizens to serve as the ultimate rulers and shapers of our democracy. As a people we know our past and we are proud of it. Our progress has been part of the living history of America, even the world. We always believed that we were part of a great movement of humanity itself called democracy, involved in the search for freedom and that belief has always strengthened us in our purpose. But just as we are losing our confidence in the future, we are also beginning to close the door on our past.

In a nation that was proud of hard work, strong families, close-knit communities, and our faith in God, too many of us now tend to worship self-indulgence and consumption. Human identity is no longer defined by what one does, but by what one owns. But we've discovered that owning things and consuming things does not satisfy our longing of meaning. We've learned that piling up material goods cannot fill the emptiness of lives which have no confidence or purpose.

The symptoms of this crisis of the American spirit are all around us. For the first time in the history of our country a majority of our people believe that the next five years will be worse than the past five years. Two-thirds of our people do not even vote. The productivity of American workers is actually dropping, and the willingness of Americans to save for the future has fallen below that of all other people in the Western world.

As you know, there is a growing disrespect for government and for churches and for schools, the news media, and other institutions. This is not a message of happiness or reassurance, but it is the truth and it is a warning.

These changes did not happen overnight. They've come upon us gradually over the last generation, years that were filled with shocks and tragedy.

We were sure that ours was a nation of the ballot, not the bullet, until the murders of John Kennedy and Robert Kennedy and Martin Luther King, Jr. We were taught that our armies were always invincible and our causes were always just, only to suffer the agony of Vietnam. We respected the Presidency as a place of honor until the shock of Watergate.

We remember when the phrase "sound as a dollar" was an expression of absolute dependability, until ten years of inflation began to shrink our dollar and our savings. We believed that our nation's resources were limitless until 1973 when we had to face a growing dependence on foreign oil.

These wounds are still very deep. They have never been healed.

Looking for a way out of this crisis, our people have turned to the Federal Government and found it isolated from the mainstream of our nation's life. Washington, D.C., has become an island. The gap between our citizens and our government has never been so wide. The people are looking for honest answers, not easy answers; clear leadership, not false claims and evasiveness and politics as usual.

What you see too often in Washington and elsewhere around the country is a system of government that seems incapable of action. You see a Congress twisted and pulled in every direction by hundreds of well-financed and powerful special interests.

You see every extreme position defended to the last vote, almost to the last breath by one unyielding group or another. You often see a balanced and a fair approach that demands sacrifice, a little sacrifice from everyone, abandoned like an orphan without support and without friends.

Often you see paralysis and stagnation and drift. You don't like it, and neither do I. What can we do?

First of all, we must face the truth, and then we can change our course. We simply must have faith in each other, faith in our ability to govern ourselves, and faith in the future of this nation. Restoring that faith and that confidence to America is now the most important task we face. It is a true challenge of this generation of Americans.

One of the visitors to Camp David last week put it this way:

"We've got to stop crying and start sweating, stop talking and start walking, stop cursing and start praying. The strength we need will not come from the White House, but from every house in America."

We know the strength of America. We are strong. We can regain our unity. We can regain our confidence. We are the heirs of generations who survived threats much more powerful and awesome than those that challenge us now. Our fathers and mothers were strong men and women who shaped a new society during the Great Depression, who fought world wars, and who carved out a new charter of peace for the world.

We ourselves are the same Americans who just ten years ago put a man on the moon. We are the generation that dedicated our society to the pursuit of human rights and equality. And we are the generation that will win the war on the energy problem and in that process rebuild the unity and confidence of America.

We are at a turning point in our history. There are two paths to choose. One is a path I've warned about tonight, the path that leads to fragmentation and self-interest. Down that road lies a mistaken idea of freedom, the right to grasp for ourselves some advantage over others. That path would be one of constant conflict between narrow interests ending in chaos and immobility. It is a certain route to failure.

All the traditions of our past, all the lessons of our heritage, all the promises of our future point to another path, the path of common purpose and the restoration of American values. That path leads to true freedom for our nation and ourselves. We can take the first steps down that path as we begin to solve our energy problem.

Energy will be the immediate test of our ability to unite this nation, and it can also be the standard around which we rally. On the battlefield of energy we can win for our nation a new confidence, and we can seize control again of our common destiny.

In little more than two decades we've gone from a position of energy independence to one in which almost half the oil we use comes from foreign countries, at prices that are going through the roof. Our excessive dependence on OPEC has already taken a tremendous toll on our economy and our people. This is the direct cause of the long lines which have made millions of you spend aggravating hours waiting for gasoline. It's a cause of the increased inflation and unemployment that we now face. This intolerable dependence on foreign oil threatens our economic independence and the very security of our nation.

The energy crisis is real. It is worldwide. It is a clear and present danger to our nation. These are facts and we simply must face them.

What I have to say to you now about energy is simple and vitally important.

Point one: I am tonight setting a clear goal for the energy policy of the United States. Beginning this moment, this nation will never use more foreign oil than we did in 1977—never. From now on, every new addition to our demand for energy will be met from our own production and our own conservation. The generation-long growth in our dependence on foreign oil will be stopped dead in its tracks right now and then reversed as we move through the 1980s, for I am tonight setting the further goal of cutting our dependence on foreign oil by one-half by the end of the next decade—a saving of over 4½ million barrels of imported oil per day.

Point two: To ensure that we meet these targets, I will use my Presidential authority to set import quotas. I'm announcing tonight that for 1979 and 1980, I will forbid the entry into this country of one drop of foreign oil more than these goals allow. These quotas will ensure a reduction in imports even below the ambitious levels we set at the recent Tokyo summit.

Point three: To give us energy security, I am asking for the most massive peacetime commitment of funds and resources in our nation's history to develop America's own alternative sources of fuel—from coal, from oil shale, from plant products for gasohol, from unconventional gas, from the sun.

I propose the creation of an energy security corporation to lead this effort to replace 2½ million barrels of imported oil per day by 1990. The corporation will issue up to $5 billion in energy bonds, and I especially want them to be in small denominations so that average Americans can invest directly in America's energy security.

Just as a similar synthetic rubber corporation helped us win World War II, so will we mobilize American determination and ability to win the energy war. Moreover, I will soon submit legislation to Congress calling for the creation of this nation's first solar bank which will help us achieve the crucial goal of 20 percent of our energy coming from solar power by the year 2000.

These efforts will cost money, a lot of money, and that is why Congress must enact the windfall profits tax without delay. It will be money well spent. Unlike the billions of dollars that we ship to foreign countries to pay for foreign oil, these funds will be paid by Americans to Americans. These funds will go to fight, not to increase, inflation and unemployment.

Point four: I'm asking Congress to mandate, to require as a matter of law, that our nation's utility companies cut their massive use of oil by 50 percent within the next decade and switch to other fuels, especially coal, our most abundant energy source.

Point five: To make absolutely certain that nothing stands in the way of achieving these goals, I will urge Congress to create an energy mobilization board which, like the War Production Board in World War II, will have the responsibility and authority to cut through the redtape, the delays, and the endless roadblocks to completing key energy projects.

We will protect our environment. But when this nation critically needs a refinery or a pipeline, we will build it.

Point six: I'm proposing a bold conservation program to involve every state, county, and city and every average American in our energy battle. This effort will permit you to build conservation into your homes and your lives at a cost you can afford.

I ask Congress to give me authority for mandatory conservation and for standby gasoline rationing. To further conserve energy, I'm proposing tonight an extra $10 billion over the next decade to strengthen our public transportation systems. And I'm asking you for your good and for your nation's security to take no unnecessary trips, to use carpools or public transportation whenever you can, to park your car one extra day per week, to obey the speed limit, and to set your thermostats to save fuel. Every act of energy conservation like this is more than just common sense—I tell you it is an act of patriotism.

Our nation must be fair to the poorest among us, so we will increase aid to needy Americans to cope with rising energy prices. We often think of conservation only in terms of sacrifice. In fact, it is the most painless and immediate way of rebuilding our nation's strength. Every gallon of oil each one of us saves is a new form of production. It gives us more freedom, more confidence, that much more control over our own lives.

So, the solution of our energy crisis can also help us to conquer the crisis of the spirit in our country. It can rekindle our sense of unity, our confidence in the future, and give our nation and all of us individually a new sense of purpose.

You know we can do it. We have the natural resources. We have more oil in our shale alone than several Saudi Arabias. We have more coal than any nation on earth. We have the world's highest level of technology. We have the most skilled work force, with innovative genius, and I firmly believe that we have the national will to win this war.

I do not promise you that this struggle for freedom will be easy. I do not promise a quick way out of our nation's problems, when the truth is that the only way out is an all-out effort. What I do promise you is that I will lead our fight, and I will enforce fairness in our struggle, and I will ensure honesty. And above all, I will act.

We can manage the short-term shortages more effectively and we will, but there are no short-term solutions to our long-range problems. There is simply no way to avoid sacrifice.

Twelve hours from now I will speak again in Kansas City, to expand and to explain further our energy program. Just as the search for solutions to our energy shortages has now led us to a new awareness of our nation's deeper problems, so our willingness to work for those solutions in energy can strengthen us to attack those deeper problems.

I will continue to travel this country, to hear the people of

America. You can help me to develop a national agenda for the 1980s. I will listen and I will act. We will act together. These were the promises I made three years ago, and I intend to keep them.

Little by little we can and we must rebuild our confidence. We can spend until we empty our treasures, and we may summon all the wonders of science. But we can succeed only if we tap our greatest resources—America's people, America's values, and America's confidence.

I have seen the strength of America in the inexhaustible resources of our people. In the days to come, let us renew that strength in the struggle for an energy-secure nation.

In closing, let me say this: I will do my best, but I will not do it alone. Let your voice be heard. Whenever you have a chance, say something good about our country. With God's help and for the sake of our nation, it is time for us to join hands in America. Let us commit ourselves together to a rebirth of the American spirit. Working together with our common faith we cannot fail.

Thank you and good night.

THE BLACK AGENDA FOR THE 1980s[1]

VERNON JORDAN JR.[2]

In spite of some gains, the decade of the seventies has not been a good one for large numbers of blacks, particularly those in the inner cities. Two recent reports, one by the National Urban League and the other by the US Civil Rights Commission, "paint a discouraging picture of little overall real progress" for blacks (*Christian Science Monitor,* Ja. 24, '80). Averages of income and employment for blacks when compared to those of whites show little gain—possibly lost ground. The hopes of black leadership when Carter took office have all but disappeared. Many blacks feel that they were not repaid for the large support they gave the Democrats in 1976.

[1] The keynote address at the Sixty-Ninth Annual Conference of the National Urban League in Chicago, Illinois, July 22, 1979. Quoted by permission.
[2] For biographical note, see Appendix.

The National Urban League, probably "the most smoothly run civil-rights organization" (Delaney, *NY Times Magazine*, Jl. 15, '79, p 22), has been of increasing importance in keeping track of the status of blacks, and its national office and research reports have received wide attention. Without a doubt, the League's president, Vernon Jordan Jr., is the most articulate black spokesman in the country and he can exercise influence with the highest levels of the nation's leadership. As a public speaker he is fluent and persuasive, ranking among the best on today's national scene. Backing his arguments with substantial evidence, he has been outspoken in recent months about the failures of the Carter administration.

The sixty-ninth annual conference of the National Urban League in Chicago, July 22–25, 1979, provided Jordan with an excellent platform from which to express his disappointment, for it attracted over 1200 people and full press coverage. The Carter administration considered it important enough to send such speakers as Secretary of State Cyrus Vance, Secretary of Labor Ray Marshall, Secretary of Treasury W. Michael Blumenthal, and Secretary of Health, Education, and Welfare Patricia Harris, as well as Rosalynn Carter and Edward Kennedy.

On the opening night, July 22, 1979, Mr. Jordan gave a fiery keynote address. After assessing the gains that had been made, he declared, "The myth of black progress is a dangerous illusion used as an excuse to halt further efforts to extend real progress to all our people." In a militant tone, he warned "aspirants to the Presidency, Democrats or Republicans alike," that "the black community will be harsh judges. Black people will be examining your record, evaluating your performance, and checking your positions."

This is the first time the National Urban League has held its Annual Conference in Chicago since 1943. It's been too long. We're glad to be here.

And we are mindful of the fact that some people asked us not to come to Chicago. Many of our friends in the Women's Movement wanted us to join their boycott of states that have not ratified the Equal Rights Amendment. After careful consideration, we decided that we had a duty to come.

Chicago is a great city whose greatness depends in part upon the fact that it is a center of black business and has the second largest black population of any American city. The Urban League has roots here. The Urban League has a constituency here. The Chicago Urban League has served the needs of the black people of Chicago since 1917. We will not ignore those needs now.

Chicago backs ERA. Chicago area state legislators support ERA. Ratification was vetoed by the same downstate politicians who dislike this city and who vote against its interests. Boycotting Chicago won't change their votes. Harming Chicago's economy won't make them hurt. Harming black businesses and workers who benefit from tourism is not a viable strategy.

So we are here in Chicago. And we will use this forum to repeat our total, complete, unequivocal, and fervent support for the Equal Rights Amendment. We are on record for ERA. A nation aspiring to full equality needs ERA. And convening here in Chicago, the National Urban League calls on the state of Illinois to ratify the Equal Rights Amendment—now.

The nation's failure to ratify ERA after so many years is a reflection of the low priority it has given to the pursuit of equality. The prime victims of that national mistrust of equality have been black people.

Twenty-five years after the *Brown* decision black Americans are assessing the fruits of that great victory. *Brown* ushered in a new era. It struck down the institution of segregation. It laid the legal, idealistic, and philosophic basis for the Second Reconstruction. It engendered realistic prospects that our nation would bring about real racial equality.

The fifteen years that followed *Brown* justified black people's faith. Real progress was made. Civil rights laws, court decisions, and executive orders changed the face of the nation. Yes, *Brown* inaugurated a new dawn in America. But the day is passed, and black people now find themselves once again in the dark midnight of persistent disadvantage.

This is not a popular view today. Many people claim that our progress has been sufficient, and that race is no longer a factor of consequence in America today.

The debate on black progress reminds me of the old question, "Is the glass half-empty or is it half-full?" The answer depends on your situation. If you are sitting on a shaded lawn next to a well-stocked cooler, the glass is half-full. But if, like the masses of black people today, you are wandering in a parched desert, that glass is not only half-empty, but it is in danger of becoming just another mirage.

Let me say firmly and clearly: There has been progress; there has been tremendous change, and more black people find themselves in better circumstances than at any time in our history. It would be dishonest to claim otherwise. Blacks in high positions have proliferated. Blacks in corporate jobs have sharply increased. Blacks are in jobs never before open to us. Blacks are in schools and colleges that never allowed us through their doors. Yes, there has been progress—for some of us.

Does that progress justify the claim that our battles are over, that the war is won? Does it justify claims that black problems are now based on class, not race? Does it justify the view that black leadership is not responsive to the changed national climate? And does it justify the claims that affirmative action and minimum wage laws harm rather than help black citizens?

As much as we celebrate the progress black people have made we must insist that the glass of our hopes is half-empty and draining fast.

The myth of black progress is a dangerous illusion used as an excuse to halt further efforts to extend real progress to all of our people. The myth of black progress illustrates the negative attitude toward blacks. It purports to show that blacks have made progress and those who have not have only themselves to blame. It sanctions the vile myth that the poor are really an underclass, incapable of being helped, unwilling to rise out of their poverty.

Let us acknowledge the great progress some of us have made. But at the same time, let us recognize the true plight in which the vast majority of black people find themselves.

Let us start with jobs. Work is the measure of a person's worth in our society. It is the key that opens all other doors. How much progress have we made in employment?

Some of us have done well. Black men and women in both

the public and the private sectors are holding job titles and receiving paychecks unheard of for black people a decade or so ago. They are solid symbols of the progress some of us have made.

But they would be the first to admit that they are visible only because of their rarity. They are exceptions. They form a small part of the black work force. The masses of black people are still in the worst jobs our society offers. Black workers are twice as likely as whites to be in low-pay, low-skill jobs, and less than half as likely as whites to be in the jobs that count in America.

The black unemployment rate is higher than it was when the *Brown* decision was handed down, and higher than it was when we marched on Washington for jobs and freedom. Black people are experiencing depression-level unemployment. With the nation now entering a new recession, black people still have not recovered from the last one.

Black youth have become an endangered, lost generation. Unemployment rates for black young people approach 60 percent in our cities. Our neo-conservative critics blame it on the minimum wage. Get rid of the minimum wage laws, they say, and black unemployment will go down.

Why then, has white youth unemployment gone down at the very time the minimum wage has gone up? Why accept the curious thesis that black jobs depend on abandoning the minimum standards of compensation every industrial nation demands? The last time black people enjoyed full employment was in 1863. There were no minimum wage laws under slavery; we'll take our chances with them today.

Income is a basic measure of progress. Some of us have made great strides. A few have reached parity with whites. We are often told about the nine percent of black families in the upper income brackets. But what about the other 91 percent? How are they doing?

A third are poor—three times the white rate. The majority are near poor. They earn less than the government itself says is needed for a minimum adequate living standard. Half a million black people were added to the ranks of the poor in the 1970s. And in this International Year of the Child the majority of black children are growing up in families experiencing severe economic hardship.

The shameful fact this nation must face is that the gap between whites and blacks is growing instead of closing. At the end of the sixties the typical black family income was 61 percent of the typical white family income. Today, it is down to 57 percent.

Education is another basic area. Twenty-five years after *Brown* more black children attend racially isolated schools than in 1954. The south has integrated its schools, the north has not. Chicago's schools are more segregated than Jackson, Mississippi's.

In some cities black high school dropouts outnumber graduates. Many school systems program black youth for failure. Many of our children spend twelve years in schools and classrooms indifferent to their fate, and then cannot pass minimum reading and arithmetic requirements.

Yes, more blacks are attending college than ever before. But the majority are in two-year community colleges while the majority of whites are in four-year schools that put them on career ladders denied to blacks. Black enrollments in medical and professional schools are declining while total enrollments rise.

Has there been progress in Housing? Some. More black families are living in decent housing, and some are living in suburbs that never saw a black face after the maid's quitting time. But the point is whether black progress is real when measured against standards enjoyed by white Americans.

By that standard, there is still an intolerable gap. One out of five black families lived in housing that the government says is physically deficient. HUD says blacks are three times as likely as whites to live in housing that has serious deficiencies. And blacks are twice as likely as whites to pay more than they can afford to get decent housing.

It is clear that the glass of racial progress is only half-full. It is clear that blacks remain disadvantaged. It is clear that race continues to be a major determining factor in our society. It is clear that, for all the progress some of us have made, half of all black Americans are boat people without boats, cast adrift in a hostile ocean of discrimination, unemployment, and poverty.

Our Conference theme is: "Mobilizing for the Challenges of the 1980s." It is to the everlasting shame of this nation that the major challenge facing it in the 1980s is the same challenge that faced it in the 1880s—the challenge of racial equality.

DuBois was right when he warned: "The problem of the Twentieth Century is the problem of the color line."

The color line is still with us. The challenge of the 1980s consists of dismantling the dehumanizing, brutalizing color line that places a ceiling on black opportunities and removes the floor from black security.

Yet, the black agenda for the 1980s is an agenda that is "black" only in the sense that blacks are disproportionately poor. It is an agenda that transcends race, sex, and region. It is an agenda directed at helping all of America's poor and deprived citizens. It is an agenda that is in the national interest.

The civil rights struggles of the 1950s and 60s concentrated on securing basic social and political rights. The struggles of the 1970s were defensive, largely limited to preserving the gains we made. Those of the 1980s must be to secure parity between blacks and whites; to remove race once and for all as a factor in determining the rewards and responsibilities in our society.

The black agenda for the 1980s starts with full employment. We reject absolutely any policies that assign poor people and black people to the role of cannon fodder in the war against inflation. We reject any unemployment goal above the bare minimum. We insist on federal compliance with the full employment mandates of the Humphrey-Hawkins Bill.

There is no ambiguity about our position. We want jobs. We want them now. We prefer them in the private sector. We'll take them in the public sector. And we're not interested in all the excuses people give why we can't have those jobs. The right to work and to earn is a basic human right. It is being denied to disproportionate numbers of black people.

Full employment and black parity in jobs implies another basic item on the black agenda: affirmative action.

The *Weber* decision removes a major obstacle to voluntary affirmative action plans. Very few government agencies or private corporations can honestly say they give minority workers a fair share of the jobs at all levels of employment. Too few can honestly demonstrate that they've made a maximum effort to do so.

After *Weber*, there can be no more excuses. The *Weber* decision clearly states that affirmative action plans can be instituted to eliminate manifest racial imbalances. The Court approved numerical goals and timetables. Employers who have been sitting on the fence, praying for a negative decision on *Weber*, will now have to get off the fence and do something about reversing the discrimination against black workers. If they don't, they can expect strong federal action and lawsuits.

We call on all public and private employers to initiate and to implement broad, vigorous affirmative action plans and to strengthen present programs designed to bring parity to black workers at all levels. If such plans are introduced this year and implemented throughout the next decade, then by 1990 we can celebrate the end of affirmative action because its goals will have been met.

And those plans must include numbers, even if some people call them quotas. No company inaugurates a marketing program without a clear idea of the sales level it wants to reach. And no company can be serious about an affirmative action plan without a clear, numerical goal.

In addressing the question of affirmative action I have stressed the private sector's role. That is no accident. It is in the private sector that we find—along with enthusiastic compliance—the strongest resistance. Four out of five jobs are in the private sector. Between 1974 and 1977—even in the midst of a recession and a weak recovery period—the American economy generated over five million new jobs. Seven out of ten were in the private sector.

Black people did not get their fair share of those jobs. In fact there was a *loss* of private sector jobs for black men in that period. While other groups, including other minorities, were expanding their share of newly created private sector jobs, black men suffered an eleven percent decline. Yes, for every ten black men with private sector jobs in 1974, only nine were employed in 1977. Jobs go up, but *our* jobs go down.

That's why we must have vigorous affirmative action. That's why affirmative action is at the top of the black agenda for the 1980s.

A humane society must provide for those who cannot work, even in a full employment economy. And in an economy where jobs are few and the jobless are many, a decent, equitable income maintenance system is a necessity.

The present welfare system is an intolerable mess. President Carter is to be commended for his attempts to get even a limited reform measure through a Congress noted for its hostility to the poor. The President's proposal can be supported only as a first step toward development of a comprehensive, federally administered income maintenance system free of punitive elements and available to all in need.

Another key item on our agenda for the 1980s is a national youth development program that would assure our young people of the skills, schooling, and services they need to participate fully in our society. The administration's current review of all federal programs that impact on youth should lead to a comprehensive national youth policy. That policy must go beyond mere coordination of existing programs to deal with the problems facing the nearly ten million black and white poor children in America. Their needs cannot be sacrificed on the altar of the balanced budget.

Health is an issue on everyone's agenda. The nation is in the midst of a debate on health care, a debate that has been personalized by the media. Black people don't care if a plan is labelled Kennedy or Carter, and our view of plans for catastrophic health insurance is that black health today is catastrophic. There is enough evidence that the Surgeon General ought to determine that being black is dangerous to your health.

Black people have limited access to quality health care. A nation concerned that it has too many doctors must realize that black neighborhoods have too few doctors. And the barely adequate public health facilities in many black neighborhoods are being closed down to balance local budgets.

The black agenda for the 1980s includes a national health system that is unified, comprehensive, consumer-oriented, and guarantees total quality health care services for all.

The black agenda also includes decent housing for all. Thirty years ago Congress passed a National Housing Act with the goal of providing "a decent home and suitable living environment for every American family." It is time to realize that goal—thirty years is long enough.

The first step toward assuring decent housing for all should be taken immediately. We favor immediate passage of the pending amendments to the Fair Housing Act of 1968. These amendments would give HUD the right to take positive steps to end housing discrimination. We call for swift passage of this new—and desperately needed—enforcement power.

The agenda for the 1980s also includes other measures such as set-asides for minority contractors, an accurate count of blacks and browns in the crucial 1980 census, and much more. But the basic, core items I have discussed here will be enough for some people to say our agenda for the 1980s is an impossible dream.

We are told this is an "era of limits," an age of "new realities." The era of scarcity is supposed to be upon us. The long lines in front of empty gas pumps are supposed to be the harbinger of the future. That's behind much of the new negativism and selfish privatism that infects our society. The guiding principle seems to be: Those who have, keep what they've got, and those who don't have, will get even less.

Last week President Carter spoke of the crisis of confi-

dence among Americans, and he rightly deplored the selfishness that pervades our society. He called on the nation to
unite in a new patriotic thrust that wages war on the energy
crisis. We support the President's call to lick the energy crisis,
but we say that energy is not a moral issue. The price of gas or
the numbers of barrels of imported oil are not the stuff of
which moral crusades are made.

Tapping the latent moral fervor of our nation and rekin-
dling the belief in American ideals needs a worthier subject.
It needs an inspiring vision—the vision of racial equality.
That is a moral issue. It is an issue still unresolved. It is an
issue that tests the moral fiber of a nation.

Our agenda for the 1980s is a battle plan for the war
against racial disadvantage and poverty. It is an agenda that
promises to revive America's heritage of idealism and its confidence in traditional values of justice, brotherhood, and
equality.

This agenda for the 1980s is feasible, necessary, and affordable. Yes, affordable. It may even be possible to finance it
through better management of available resources.

When it comes to poor people's programs, Congress is
quick to cut back. It cries fraud when high food prices mean
spending more on food stamps. When affluent doctors rip off
Medicaid patients Congress blames the victims. When sharp
operators play games with youth jobs programs Congress
blames the kids.

But when the government gets ripped off for billions in
military cost overruns, it just goes back and writes a bigger
check. Last January the Comptroller General issued a report
on cost overruns for federal hardware. The amounts are staggering. Federal cost overruns amounted to over $200 billion.
Eliminating those cost overruns and pork barrel projects and
squeezing waste out of current programs could yield billions
for the agenda for the 1980s.

Our agenda for the 1980s is not an impossible dream. It is
a matter of priorities. It is a matter of leadership and resource
management.

America's public and private leadership suffers from a

cramped view of its responsibilities. Few exhibit the quality of leadership as defined by Professor James McGregor Burns, who writes:

Truly great and creative leaders . . . arouse people's hopes and aspirations and expectations, convert social needs into political demands, and rise to higher levels of leadership as they respond to those demands.

Leadership, says Burns,

is power governed by principle, directed toward raising people to their highest levels of personal motive and social morality and tested by the achieving of results measured by the original purpose.

By that definition, our nation faces a crisis of leadership and a crisis of confidence in that leadership. That crisis is primarily political, but it infects private leadership as well. Given a cautious administration and a hostile Congress, there is a need for men and women in the private and voluntary sectors to come forth with the leadership that inspires the great creativity of this nation.

Black citizens have a responsibility to encourage that kind of leadership. We must exercise our moral claims on the nation through pressure on public and private leaders. We must develop the political strength that will ensure greater responsiveness by elected officials.

It will be crucial for black leadership to follow sound strategies in the coming campaign for the Presidency. It is too early for black people to become enmeshed in speculation on who to support or to run informal primaries in the black community. It is too early for blacks to call for dumping Carter, drafting Kennedy or backing Baker. There's too much at stake for black people to become pawns in other people's games.

The black strategy should be to hang loose and make the candidates come to us. No one can win without the black vote. The black vote is not in anyone's pocket. It must not be given away; it must be earned with ironclad commitments to the programs and policies black people need.

It's a long, grueling road to the White House. Whoever climbs that rocky road is going to have to make plenty of stops before he makes the victory statement. He's going to have to make stops with Democrats, with Republicans, with Independents, with business and labor, with women, and most assuredly, with black and brown people.

Anyone who hopes to be called "Mr. President" in 1981 is going to have to come by here. He'll have to make stops in Chicago's South Side, in Atlanta's West Side, in Harlem, in Watts, and in the urban and rural strongholds of black voters. Yes, no matter who he is, incumbent or challenger, he's got to come by here.

Any candidate who ignores us is in jeopardy. Any candidate who takes us for granted is in double jeopardy.

To Mr. Carter, we say—"remember the black vote." It put you in the Oval Office. Ninety-four percent of black voters cast their ballot for you. They swung the South behind you. They were your margin of victory in key northern states. But the enthusiasm of black voters has cooled. There is disappointment in the black community.

Black citizens understand that the process of governance means compromise and delay. But they understand too, that their rights and needs have been compromised and delayed since the birth of our nation.

Black people appreciate your urban programs but they're not enough. Black people appreciate your job efforts, but they're not enough. Black people appreciate your health and welfare plans, but they're not enough. Black people appreciate your appointments of blacks to judgeships and other high posts—but they're just not enough.

The expectation of bold leadership and renewed moral commitment to minority needs has not been fulfilled.

We understand a President has the right to determine who shall serve in his administration. But we watch with great interest to see what effect these changes will have on our needs, our aspirations and our agenda for the 1980s.

To all other aspirants to the Presidency, Democrats or Republicans alike, the black community will be harsh judges.

Black people will be examining your record, evaluating your performance, and checking your positions.

In the meantime, it is the responsibility of the black community to maximize black registration and voter turnout. We don't have the wealth. We don't have the power. But we do have the numbers. Those numbers won't count unless we register and vote. The black agenda for the 1980s depends on that.

Because black voting rates are so low we have Congressmen who vote against our interests. Right now those Congressmen are trying to repeal the *Brown* decision through a constitutional amendment to ban busing. The Mottl Amendment will prevent black kids from getting equal educational opportunities. It must be defeated.

While we strengthen black voting power we also must strengthen the black-brown coalition. And we must revive the traditional coalitions that share our agenda for the 1980s.

Black people know that freedom is not free. We know that we've bought the little we have at a dear price, a price paid over centuries of oppression and misery, a price paid through painful stuggle and constant agitation. Yes, we know the truth of Frederick Douglass' immortal words:

If there is no struggle, there is no progress. Those who profess to favor freedom and yet deprecate agitation are men who want crops without plowing up the ground, they want rain without thunder and lightning. They want the ocean without the awful roar of its many waters.

Black people understand the struggle for equality. We know we must weather the storms ahead—storms of recession, of racism, of an uncaring nation. Yes, we know our days of sacrifice and struggle are not over.

Our struggle is for America's soul. We know that our struggle is one to revive the floundering moral principles of our nation. We have faith in America's ideals, in her promises of equality, in her innate morality. Our faith has been sorely tried, it has been burned in the furnace of racial hatreds, but always, black people have revived their faith in America and through their example and commitment, America's faith in itself.

We say to our beloved nation, in the words of the Roman poet [Virgil]:

> The descent to hell is easy
> The gates stand open day and night
> But to reclimb the slope
> And escape to the upper air
> That is labor . . .

Take the hard path, America. Climb the slopes of justice and freedom and equality for all. Breathe the freedom of the upper air, America, the clean fresh air of morality and commitment.

Yes, we call on all of the people of this great nation to come together and unite behind an agenda for the 1980s that will make this the most progressive, the most inspiring decade in our history.

Now, let us at this Annual Conference of the National Urban League work to that end. Let us begin the labor that will help take America to a new era of righteousness, truth, and equality. Let us do our part to make America an open, integrated, pluralistic society where freedom rings and justice flourishes.

THE BROWN DECISION, PLURALISM, AND THE SCHOOLS IN THE 1980s[1]

HAROLD HOWE II [2]

Today educators face myriad problems, the solutions to many of which are beyond their control. Turmoil has come from many directions: resistance to forced busing for racial balance; shifting school population because of flight to suburbs, the practice of af-

[1] Delivered at the 1979 Summer Institute of the Chief State School Officers of the United States, at Smuggler's Notch, Jeffersonville, Vermont, 8:30 A.M. August 1, 1979. Quoted by permission.
[2] For biographical note, see Appendix.

fluent parents placing children in private schools; attempts to
meet the special educational needs of the culturally and economic-
ally disadvantaged, minorities, and women; violence and vandal-
ism by students; demands for teacher competency tests and better
textbooks; "teacher burnout" under intense classroom pressure;
the decline in student achievement scores; teacher militancy for
higher pay and better classroom conditions; and last, proposals for
tax limitations (such as Proposition Thirteen in California).

When he spoke to the Chief State School Officers' 1979 Summer Institute, held at Smuggler's Notch, Jeffersonville, Vermont,
August 1, 1979, Harold Howe II, Vice President of the Ford Foundation and a former US Commissioner for Education (1965–68),
hoped to provide the men and women who head the 56 state and
territorial school systems with a perspective, an overall view of
why the schools are facing so many difficult problems. The audience was a select one for it included only "chiefs" (no deputies or
alternates were invited).

Howe notes that the commitment to human rights, of which
school integration is a part, has also brought contrary demands
from minority groups to preserve their racial identity or native
languages. Standing firm in his advocacy of equal opportunity,
Howe suggests a better blending of the "melting pot theory"
(Americanization) and pluralism so that both can be interwoven
and accommodated within our system of education. He warns,
however that "we are engaged in a long, difficult struggle with intractable and multifaceted difficulties. . . . There is no quick fix."

Those interested in reading another speech by Howe will find
his address "Public Education for a Humane Society," in *Representative American Speeches: 1972–1973.*

The myths we live by are often more significant than the
facts of our lives. In the United States we have changed our
myths in your lifetime and mine. When most of us gathered
here went to elementary school, one prevailing myth about
America and Americans was faith in the melting pot, a term
for which we are indebted to Israel Zangwill, who wrote at
the turn of the century, "America is God's Crucible, the
Great Melting Pot where all races of Europe are melting and
reforming." We saw ourselves and our fellow Americans as
persons with strong common denominators based on a common history, on a common and somewhat simplistic patriotism, and on the hope of success in a land that had provided

freedom and opportunity to many. We believed that those who joined us from abroad—ordinarily Europe—might have trouble getting started in America, but we were sure from the experience of past generations that the benign action of the melting pot would soon turn them into "real" Americans, who shared the traditions and beliefs of the rest of us and who would start climbing the ladder of success as soon as they were Americanized.

Most of us conveniently forgot that persons with black skins, Hispanics whose ancestors may have arrived here before our own, and native Americans were exceptions to this myth, and those who remembered this unpleasant fact tended to regard it as an exception rather than a denial of the myth. Persons who insisted on preserving their native language and culture were seen as almost un-American. If they chose this foolish course, we were not to blame for the troubles they encountered in America. Persons whose ancestors had been slaves were subjected to official and unofficial discrimination. Native Americans had suffered a special kind of inequality to which we had grown accustomed. Many states in our Union maintained ingenious ways to deprive blacks, Hispanics, and native Americans of political, economic, and personal rights even though the Constitution under which we all lived forbade discrimination on the basis of race, religion, or national origin.

Our parents' vision of the myth in those years of our own elementary education saw the schools as the main device for heating the melting pot, particularly the schools of the cities. Under their influence, the illiterate would become literate, the foreign would become American and shed their strangeness, and the bottom rungs of the ladder of success would become available to most everyone. It was a comforting view, that made us feel good about our land and ourselves. It's too bad it was only half true, with enough misconceptions and errors to warrant labelling it a myth.

Today we have a new and different myth that grows in part from our national experience in the 1960s and 1970s. It is called pluralism, and its main feature is denial of the melting

pot. Now American society is seen by many as a loose association of competing groups, each of which makes a first claim
on the loyalty and interest of its members—a claim so strong
that it often supersedes or ignores the common denominators
that hold us together as one people. We have become a nation of minorities, each emphasizing its race or its language or
its culture or its national origin or some combination of these.
Of course, pluralism as an idea for characterizing American
society has been around for a long time, but only recently has
it gained ascendency over the melting pot.

The schools are caught up in this new myth, just as they
were in the old one. Under a decision of the Supreme Court,
the language of a minority must be recognized in the schools,
and we have invented bilingual education, a concept to
which we give numerous definitions depending on the characteristics of the group and sometimes of the individual. Various
groups demand that the curriculum of the schools recognize
their past history and their cultural interests, and the schools
regard it as their duty to respond. Group loyalties are so powerful that they impel people to deny the dream of an integrated school and an integrated society and to stick together
in relative isolation, even though this may ultimately defeat
the aspiration most people have for joining the mainstream of
economic success and the guarantee of individual rights.

The *Brown* decision and the developments that flowed
from it powerfully influenced the transition from one myth to
the other, less as a result of the specific arguments of the decision itself than of the forces it awakened in the land, forces
that gathered strength rapidly in the 1950s, deeply affected
our national life in the 1960s, and solidified themselves in recent years. While the legal impact of the *Brown* decision was
to overturn the doctrine of "separate but equal," stemming
from the earlier Court ruling in *Plessy vs Ferguson* in 1896, its
real impact was in the assertion that racial characteristics are
unacceptable in the United States as a basis for decisions of
government about people. It proclaimed the end of second-
class citizenship and called for equality in the broadest sense.
More than that, it said to millions of Americans, who had

been officially discriminated against, not only that they were
equal to their oppressors but also that they had some right to
redress of wrongs from those same parties. It qualified that
right of redress by saying it could not be expected immediately but "with all deliberate speed," whatever that meant.
In effect *Brown* said, you can't have two melting pots, one for
Europeans and one for others who will be kept separate.

Armed with this elusive promise of equality, blacks, Hispanics, and some others set out to capture the rights they had
been promised but denied, and they found it no easy task. No
one was going to give them their newly defined legal rights on
a platter. They would have to fight for them in busses, at
lunch counters, at voter registration offices, with school
boards, in state legislatures, in the United States Congress,
and in the courts. The fight was to be long and frustrating and
bitter, and it is not over yet. Nor will it be when you and I
pass on our responsibilities for education to another generation.

An important by-product of that long and bitter fight was
the increased solidarity of the minority groups engaged in it.
The frustrations encountered by blacks, Hispanics, and native
Americans as they attempted to claim rights that were legally
theirs but denied them in practice turned them back to their
own fellowship for psychological sustenance. Only a few of
them succeeded in joining the mainstream, in making the
transition to the middle class, or in attaining a true rapport
that could be described as integration with the dominant
white group. In effect the melting pot remained a concept for
European immigrants rather than for our country's oldest minorities.

These experiences fertilized the seeds of pluralism, a doctrine that proclaims quite correctly that a person's race and
heritage and language are qualities to be proud of and to
draw strength from rather than to be denied and rejected.
The "Black is Beautiful" emphasis through which we passed
in the 1960s, was an exaggerated but necessary phase of this
phenomenon. Other examples were black, Hispanic, and
other studies introduced almost overnight in schools and col-

leges. They frequently were ill-conceived and ill-taught, and they sometimes resulted in denial of a solid education for young people; but they met a deep need for self-definition and self-respect in minority groups. Still another example was the demand of blacks for black dormitories and social centers on college campuses that surprised many white college presidents, who thought that integration was what minority persons should want.

As blacks, Hispanics, and native Americans began to make some gains through their newly effective solidarity, other ethnic groups in American society had two reactions. First, they resented the competition of the older minorities, particularly at the transition point from government-supported poverty to economic independence. They saw more blacks making that transition and believed, rightly in some instances, that blacks' economic ascent challenged their own. Secondly, they saw that this kind of change was possible for blacks and for some Hispanics because they were organized into groups that could bring leverage on government and get results.

These two lessons combined to denigrate the melting pot as the model for success in America, and various groups joined the pluralist bandwagon as the route to their own salvation. In effect they said "the hell with waiting around to be assimilated into the mainstream; we must organize and get ours quicker, just as the blacks are doing."

At this point I am prepared to concede that the foregoing is a simplistic interpretation of a complex series of events. I am prepared also to argue that there is enough validity to it to use it as a taking-off point for talking about what our schools need to consider as they plan their strategies for serving American society in the years ahead. The 1980s will be a time when our schools must revive some of the virtues of the melting pot, reduce some of the excesses of pluralism, and blend these two together in a new vision of American society that seeks simultaneously to identify important common denominators for all our people, while recognizing the richness and value of the many traditions and cultures from which Americans claim major elements of their strength and their satisfaction.

You may want to argue that these two concepts are fundamentally opposed and that we must go one way or the other—that we cannot be many peoples and one people at the same time. In response to this, I say only that we can if we will try hard enough. The same type of argument is frequently made about education in America, when it is asserted that we cannot achieve an educational system that has both excellence and equality as its major characteristics. I submit, however, that a fair look at the evidence suggests we have gone a long way in our schools and colleges toward achieving these twin purposes simultaneously. Right now we are going through a phase of attempting to repair the quality of excellence in our schools, just as we went through a phase in the 1960s of emphasis on openness and equal opportunity. Today we too easily forget that each succeeding generation of Americans has been more literate than its predecessor; and in our enthusiasm for repairing evident shortcomings in the schools, we forget also their great achievements in providing this society with an educated citizenry.

So it is possible in America to fit together into a working whole strong trends that have some elements of opposition. It takes persistence, good judgment, and firm resistance to the temptations of extremism. It places special strains on leaders, who must avoid over-reacting to the cyclical swings of reform movements and losing a sense of balance.

A society that succeeds in balancing the claims of pluralism and the melting pot will be like a smoothly working jazz combo [Riesman's analogy]. The instrumentalists merge their playing to create their music, which is then powerfully augmented and enriched as one after another—the pianist, the drummer, the trumpeter, the saxophonist, and the bass player—performs in his personal and unique style with a solid background from the rest of the group. One may shine more than another; if he can, so be it. But the set always ends with a flourish in which all are interwoven and with a result that is greater than the sum of the solo parts.

The fact of racial differences in America has placed a greater strain on the myth of the melting pot than any other of the factors that occasionally divide our people. And the same fact has created a dilemma for the concept of pluralism, which to be workable at all must assume that groups seeking to preserve their identity will have equal opportunity, not only for group status but also for the individual standing of group members in the larger society. During most of our history, we have denied equality in status both to racially identifiable groups and to individuals from those groups. It was the *Brown* decision that pulled us up short by asserting that race was unacceptable as a basis for decisions by government about Americans.

This past history casts its shadow over all of us every day of our lives. We cannot escape it. It tests our moral fiber, our idealism, and our commitment to what we say we believe. When we hold up a mirror and look at ourselves honestly, that shadow dominates our reflection.

Nowhere is the strain and stress of living in this shadow more evident than in those institutions which serve the coming generation and to which we commit a large proportion of our hopes for the future, the elementary and secondary schools. We depend fundamentally on the schools, both to pass on to our children the civilization we have inherited, as well as to create in them the wit and the will to continually reshape that civilization closer to our ideas than we have. In spite of the studies of some social scientists, who contend that education is unable to overcome the handicaps of racial discrimination and economic disadvantage, and in spite of the claims of a few theorists who argue that traits of mind and motivation are innate and immutable, Americans generally remain committed to the view that we can create schools with the capacity to move people out of the shadows of the past and into a new era of light. While that commitment has wavered some in recent years, it generally remains strong. We will allow it to erode at our peril.

For the twenty-five years since the *Brown* decision, a significant arena for testing our commitment to fairness in

American society has been the embattled issue of school de-segregation. There are other important elements in the long American march to a just society, including issues about employment opportunities and political rights on which some progress has been made, but the central concern for educators and an important continuing challenge for all Americans is ridding our schools of the taint of racism. We have made some progress on this front also, but we have a long way to go before we are anywhere near the dream that was so power-fully enunciated from the steps of the Lincoln Memorial in Washington by Martin Luther King in 1963.

This is not the place for a history of the ebb and flow of the contest over school desegregation. Most of you have lived through it and have vivid memories, as I do, of victories and defeats, of pursuing what turned out to be simplistic and in-effective solutions, and of fashioning remedies for segregation and racial isolation that placed the burden of redressing these wrongs more heavily on their victims than on the perpetra-tors. There was rarely a better contest for Monday morning quarterbacking than the contest over desegregation of the schools.

We have learned some hard lessons from our experience with school desegregation in the years since the *Brown* deci-sion, although we are not always willing to admit it. The two most important lessons of the first twenty-five years since *Brown* should shape our thinking as we plan our course for the 1980s:

> *First*, the forces in American society that bring about segregated living and produce racial isolation in neigh-borhoods and schools are not within the control of the schools nor of the authorities that operate them, al-though those authorities sometimes align themselves with these forces rather than opposing them. These forces stem on the one hand from private decision-mak-ing that is too often motivated by well-disguised racial prejudice and on the other from government programs in housing, transportation, and other areas of national pol-

icy with objectives unrelated to education but with powerful if unintended effects on where people live and where their children go to school.

Second, it is simplistic to believe, as many of us did well into the 1960s, that merely bringing together in school children from minority and white majority backgrounds will, in and of itself, provide minority children with the special opportunities they need to move out of the shadow of more than a hundred years of legal and illegal discrimination.

The first of these lessons about the forces that encourage racial isolation in the living patterns of our cities and suburbs should make us rethink our long-term strategy for school desegregation in the years ahead. It is just plain unrealistic to expect that solely by litigation and its resulting court orders for a variety of traditional remedies such as magnet schools, busing, redistricting, pairing of schools and the like, we can devise a permanent solution to the school desegregation problems of the massive concentrations of minority group people collected in our largest cities. Nor is it reasonable to assume that enforcement action by HEW under Title VI of the Civil Rights Act can do much more than nibble at the edges of such problems.

I do not want to be misunderstood on this point, for I am not advocating the end of busing, the curtailment of litigation, or any decline in the energy with which HEW pursues its duty to enforce the law. All these activities must continue. They are the best medicines we can prescribe now for the disease of segregated urban schools. They bring some change and some progress, and in some smaller cities they offer real hope of beneficial change. But in the most difficult situations, they are palliatives rather than cures. It is possible that litigation seeking metropolitan solutions that include suburban and central city school systems in common desegregation plans may be of major help, but so far the federal courts have been wary of this approach.

There are, however, important possibilities for a more

comprehensive, long-term strategy directed at avoiding the condition of two separate societies—one white and one black and Hispanic—or perhaps even three separate societies, with the rapidly growing proportion of Hispanics settled in enclaves of linguistic and cultural separatism—a development which holds the danger for the United States of its own Spanish-speaking version of the Canadian experience in Quebec. Such a strategy might be forged by bringing together in the courts, in enforcement actions through the administrative departments of government, and in various incentive schemes, the multiple concerns about racial discrimination in schools, in housing, and in other areas.

In recent months the Justice Department has reorganized its efforts to attack discrimination in education and in housing by bringing these two usually separate fields under the same office in its Civil Rights Division. The possibility of school desegregation suits with fair housing litigation worked into them to bring the federal courts into these two clearly related issues at the same time is already being explored in the Justice Department.

On the administrative enforcement front under the requirements of the 1964 and 1968 Civil Rights Acts, it should be possible to devise joint administrative enforcement actions by HUD and HEW, although the idea of two separate departments cooperating in such a politically volatile task probably isn't practical without an initiative from the President to tell them to do so. Desegregation of schools or housing or anything else is not a popular subject with any President, and the last three of them have managed to avoid it most of the time. It is unpopular because it is a loser in the political sense; you stand to lose more votes than you gain by insisting that racial minorities enjoy their constitutional rights to non-discriminatory housing and schooling. But what if a President had enough vision to see that a new long-term strategy linking housing policies and school desegregation might enable him to suggest the possibility of reducing court orders requiring busing and of eventually reducing the need for busing to give children their constitutional rights? It seems to me that such a promise might be turned into a political asset. Right now when the former Secretary of HUD has just become the Secretary of HEW isn't a bad time to consider joint approaches to discrimination in education and housing.

Incentive programs can be conceived that don't require racial integration but that reward it sufficiently to make city planners, school authorities, and even individual families think twice about foregoing the economic benefits offered for desegregated schools and housing. I shall not attempt to stipulate the details of such programs, but I do believe that they constitute a relatively unexplored area. We have something of the kind now in what is called Emergency School Assistance for school districts that are actively desegregating and have need for special funds. Preferences for housing loans both in terms of who gets them and the rate of interest might encourage some movement away from racial concentrations and toward integrated living patterns. Certainly we need to recognize that the record of federally supported housing authorities in creating the ghettos of America is not a proud one, and we should find ways to turn their influence in more constructive directions. I wonder if anyone has thought of requiring the new and popular tax free bonds issued by cities and towns for private housing mortgages to satisfy a test of racial integration before receiving approval of tax exemption.

To sum up these observations on new initiatives in school desegregation, let me quote from a letter [June 27, 1979] I received from Paul Dimond, one of the attorneys involved in the recent *Columbus* and *Dayton* cases before the Supreme Court, and a person with a significant record in seeking both constitutional rights and better education for the children in our schools.

In all our thinking about new initiatives, however, I don't think we should ever let HUD, HEW, Commerce, and Justice off the hook easily. They do have large program and enforcement responsibilities that could be coordinated and redirected in a fashion that is consistent with ending the process of segregation. I don't accept as inevitable, for example, that HUD programs must aid middle income-persons to be consistent with integration objectives; that HUD, Commerce, and HEW low-income and urban revitalization efforts must perpetuate segregation rather than promote integration; that the Justice Department must forever rely solely on litigation, rather than including administrative oversight and coordination, because of the in-bred biases of some lawyers; that Title VI, Title VII, or Title VIII [Civil Right Acts of 1964 and 1968] must inevitably slip into disrepute from lack of creative implementation and failure to date to establish any substantive standards. Better federal policy and action in these areas is politically feasible and administratively workable; and it certainly is not inconsistent with grass-roots and incentive approaches. We can and should ask more of the Carter Administration and its successor administrations, even while building a better political climate and developing and targeting some creative and effective incentive efforts and enforcement strategies for integration.

Turning to the second of our hard-won lessons on school desegregation, what can be said about the paucity of evidence that school desegregation has so far produced large-scale improvements in measurable learning among black children? We are in about the same place in studying the effects of school desegregation that we were in studying the significance of class size twenty years ago. We have slowed up the process of making newly designed studies from basic data and started to do studies of past studies.

The most recent of these by Robert Crain and Rita Mahard of the Rand Corporation shows that 73 studies of school desegregation found positive effects on black achievement in 40, negative effects in 12, and no effects at all in 21 for a generally positive picture of the learning effects of school desegregation as contrasted with more negative views expressed earlier by the renowned James Coleman, the partiarch among analytical scholars of racial differences in schools.

I don't expect much more insight from studies like these than is already available to us. By and large, the finer points of interpretation that emerge from the regression equations used by sophisticated analysts are of more use to scholars for the conduct of arguments with each other than they are to teachers, principals, and school superintendents for improving education. Nor are these studies much use to those whose obligation it is to enforce the law and to bring students their constitutional right to desegregated schools. As I shall point out in more detail in a moment, the constitutional obligation to desegregate the schools has little or nothing to do with the learning outcomes of meeting such requirements.

About all that can be said now about the effects of desegregation is that sometimes it helps learning and sometimes it doesn't; probably more often than not, it does. The mechanisms by which desegregation is introduced into schools and classrooms determine the consequences for learning. But the naive hope some of us had that desegregating the schools would rapidly remove the learning differences between blacks and whites turns out to be exactly what it was, naive. As the Carnegie Council on Children underlined for us in its 1977 report, *All Our Children* [by Kenneth Keniston], the handicaps inherent in the economic conditions, health, and other disadvantages suffered by poor and minority families are fundamental causes of inequality that can limit the child's capacity to take advantage of the traditional school program.

But this does not mean that educators should either give up in despair while awaiting the advent of economic equity or reduce their efforts to improve and desegregate the schools. About the only help that educators can get from social scientists is the realization that the job they are trying to do is more complex than they expected. In a sense, this is real help because it allows them to deal with reality rather than with unrealistic hopes. But in terms of what to do that is different from what they are doing and that might make a difference, educators are pretty much on their own. They will have to draw on hunches, on very limited evidence from research, and more than anything else on their own notions of what is right. Using such sources as my guide, I want to bring these observations to a close with some suggestions for those responsible for the schools in the 1980s.

First of all, don't be deterred from desegregating the schools because doing so seems to have limited effects on test scores in reading and mathematics. That is not what school desegregation is all about, at least in the first instance. The constitutional requirement to desegregate where there is evidence of discrimination by public authority was established by the Supreme Court in 1954 and reiterated by it a month ago in the *Dayton* and *Columbus* cases. It has nothing to do with tests, achievement levels, or other scorekeeping by educators. It is instead a prohibition of racial discrimination by official bodies. As James Coleman himself once said, "Let's suppose the 1966 research of mine (*Equality of Educational Opportunity*) had come out with the opposite conclusion—namely, that black children did worse in predominantly middle-class schools. Should the courts have used that as an argument? I cannot envision a decision saying that segregation is constitutionally required because black children do better in segregated classrooms" [NY *Times*, Ag. 24 '75].

I would add to James Coleman's assertion opposing official discrimination that constitutional rights cannot and should not be conditioned by student performance. We assure freedom for the press in our constitution and suffer numerous abuses from the fourth estate in order to preserve it. Freedom of religion allows many practices that a majority of Americans would at best consider foolish. Why do we insist that the constitutional right to freedom from racial discrimination by public authority makes no sense unless it produces better reading scores?

But if we desegregate the schools to give children their constitutional rights regardless of the learning outcomes, we still have the overwhelmingly important job of doing something about the latter. It is probably true that the deprivations of poverty and racial discrimination over long years cannot be entirely overcome by the schools alone. Nevertheless, there are enough instances of success by skilled teachers working in alliance with parents who care and with the encouragement of dedicated principals to make me think that the schools can do considerably more than they are now doing. And the gains that the schools can make are not dependent upon completing the process of desegregation, although that can help to some degree. In addition to meeting our legal obligations we must learn to use the talent we have in America's schools to raise the skills and the morale of those teachers and principals who now find their task unmanageable and their jobs frustrating.

I suspect that one reason for the decline in morale and the growth of discouragement among school teachers has been the vote of no confidence they have received from the political representatives of the American people. I know of no profession that has been harassed to the same degree by politicians, who have decided to take into their own hands the details of a complex business, teaching and learning, that these same politicians know very little about. They have imposed state laws about the accountability of teachers and the testing of children that intrude into the educational process in unforeseen ways. The bandwagon of basic competency testing has spread so rapidly that it is hard to find a state without this unproved nostrum as its main answer to the improvement of teaching and learning.

You and I know that educational measurement carefully and properly used has some value in a school improvement program, and we know also that without a much larger investment in ensuring quality of instruction it has little value and is probably a deterrent to learning. I wonder why we have allowed this wave of muddle headed thinking and ill-informed action to break over us? Overemphasis on tests is analogous to a medical procedure that consists solely of diagnosis without ever prescribing a remedy. In addition, most of the testing now being required is useless for defining the remedy needed for an individual child.

In schools which have undergone formal desegregation there is a special opportunity because the process of desegregating shakes things up and offers the chance to rethink organization, curriculum, and other fundamental elements of the school's program. Where this opportunity is grasped imaginatively, there is research evidence that learning improves.

All this suggests that we will have to spend the 1980s fashioning programs in every school to help teachers to be more successful with children. Such efforts can succeed. They depend upon learning how to take into account the beliefs, attitudes, and culture that children bring to school with them.

They depend also upon working with children as individuals, maintaining high expectations in school for all the children there, building links between the school and the home, providing resources to help teachers with difficult problems, strengthening principals' skills as instructional leaders, and turning our energies in educational research from large-scale surveys of highly analyzed data to careful observation and illumination of the intimate business of teaching and learning that occurs between teacher and child.

In support of these assertions, I call to your special attention the recent research in London by Michael Rutter and his colleagues [*Fifteen Thousand Hours: Secondary Schools and Their Effects on Children*]. They appear to me to be well on the way to proving that schools with certain characteristics can and do make a difference to so-called disadvantaged students, and to proving in addition that the factors in schools that matter most in determining their capacity for positive influences on "pupils' behavior, attendance, exam success, and delinquency" are "the characteristics of schools as social institutions." Their study concludes "that schools can do much to foster good behavior and attainments, and that even in a disadvantaged area, schools can be a force for good."

These are refreshing assertions in the face of the oversimplified generalizations that the United States media have popularized to the effect that schools don't make a difference. As I have noted earlier, schools may not be able all on their own to overcome all the effects of poverty and discrimination, but there is clear evidence in Rutter's research that they can be much more effective in moving toward this goal if they are properly organized and operated. This will come as no news to many teachers and principals, but it may surprise a few social scientists, who are accustomed to judging the schools by reading computer printouts rather than visiting them. This is like studying matrimony by reading the divorce statistics.

Bringing about a commitment to these purposes in our schools cannot be legislated by state or national government. It is more the business of local school boards and local superintendents and still more the concern of principals and teachers. But state and national governments can help in two ways—by providing funds and by refraining from writing detailed prescriptions about how they are to be used. The best rethinking and reform of practice in the schools will come from persons who encounter children every day, not from persons removed from that experience.

Back in 1967 the Congress and the President created the Education Professions Development Act to provide resources for the retraining of teachers and other educational personnel. The core of this legislation was allowed to lapse in 1975. Although it had some imperfections, we need something like it in the 1980s. Also, we need to recognize in states and local districts that funds from Title I of the Elementary and Secondary Education Act, the really large-scale source of federal money for schools, can be turned to the same purposes. In addition, schools need more freedom than they are now allowed to combine funds from different sources for the benefit of children in the classroom. The concept that the numerous federal programs for assistance to education must be separate and discrete in the school is a prescription for educational chaos.

In conclusion I return to where this discussion began, to the myths we live by. One of those myths is that Americans can solve any problem in short order if only they will turn their energies to the task. The experience of the past twenty years in the schools with the related issues of school desegregation and school improvement should by now have convinced us that as far as the schools are concerned, this is indeed a myth. We are engaged in a long, difficult struggle with intractable and multi-faceted difficulties. We shall still be so engaged at the onset of the 1990s. There is no quick fix.

But in the ten years ahead of us we have a chance to make some progress. That chance depends upon tempering our attitudes toward both pluralism and the melting pot in ways that will allow us to draw strength from both, upon rethinking our obligations and our strategies for bringing children their constitutional rights under the *Brown* decision, and upon school reform fundamentally based on the exchange between teachers and children.

THE PRESS AND THE LAW

CONCILIATION BETWEEN THE PRESS AND THE LAW[1]

WILLIAM J. BRENNAN JR.[2]

The dedication of the S.I. Newhouse Center for Law and Justice at Rutgers University in downtown Newark (NJ) provided an excellent forum for consideration of the relations of the press to the courts. The Center, a refurbished 15-story office building, was made possible through a $1.5 million grant to the University from the S.I. Newhouse Foundation, founded by the head of one of the nation's largest communications firms that includes a 29 newspaper chain in 11 states. Among the audience of 1,000 were many national and local leaders. Other speakers included Irving R. Kaufman, Chief Justice of the Second Circuit Court of Appeals in New York; Rutgers University President Edward J. Bloustein; and Newark Mayor Kenneth Gibson.

The selection of William J. Brennan Jr., Associate Justice of the US Supreme Court, to give a principal address at the dedication was a fortunate choice, for he is a native son of Newark and practiced law there from 1931 to 1949. He has been a member of the Court since 1956, during a period when it has become increasingly involved in "freedom of the press" rulings. On First Amendment matters Justice Brennan is recognized as a friend of the press and has voted with the minority on many recent decisions involving restraints on the freedoms of the Fourth Estate.

Stressing the interdependence of the Court and the press, he detects "a new and disturbing note of acrimony, almost bitterness in the hostility of the press toward recent decisions" (*Herbert vs Lando*, and *Garnett Co. Inc. vs DePasquale*) and suggests that "in the heat of controversy the press may be misapprehending the issue at stake."

In his speech, Brennan draws a distinction between what the press according to the First Amendment may say ("speech model") and its actual ability to gather and disseminate the news in the

[1] Delivered at the dedication of Samuel I. Newhouse Law Center, Rutgers University, Newark, New Jersey, October 17, 1979. Title supplied by editor. Quoted by permission.
[2] For biographical note, see Appendix.

face of competing interests ("structural model"). He thinks that
many of the problems stem from press confusion between the two
models. In the matter of competing interests, it is primarily a
question, he says, of "whether the press' ability to perform the
communications functions required by our democratic society
would be significantly impaired if an editorial privilege were not
created." He notes that application of the First Amendment is far
from certain in as yet "uncharted domains."

The speech, legalistic in its development and language, is intended for the sophisticated listener and lawyers familiar with
constitutional guarantees of freedom of press and the implications
of recent court decisions. In consideration of his audience and to
authenticate his statements, he carefully documented all of his references to cases and publications. (In the printed version, the exact
citations are inserted.)

The Washington *Post* (O. 18, '79) called the speech "unusually
forceful."

My presence here today at the dedication of the Samuel I.
Newhouse Law Center is something of a coming home. I was
born in Newark. I grew up and was educated in this city. My
father was Director of Public Safety for 13 years during the
time Newark was governed by a five-member City Commission. But I also have particular ties to this building. I practiced law in Newark and the American Insurance Company,
of which I was a Director for some years, was one of my firm's
clients. So as Director and counsel I spent many hours and
days in this building over a good many years. You will appreciate then why there is special meaning for me in its rebirth
as the Samuel I. Newhouse Law Center to stand, as the university observes, "as a symbol of the growth and redevelop-
ment of the city, expressing faith and confidence in Newark
and its role as an important hub for higher education in New
Jersey."

This marvelous Center is made possible by the Samuel I.
Newhouse Foundation. We were all deeply distressed by the
recent death of Mr. Newhouse. Mr. Newhouse was one of the
legendary figures of American newspapers; he was the founder of the Newhouse chain, the flagship of which is Newark's
own *Star Ledger*. It is eminently appropriate that Mr. New-

house, who did so much to facilitate communication across
the tribal barriers that divide our society, should have been
instrumental in providing the facilities that will foster similar
communication among the various departments of legal education.

Although I am unabashedly local and take a partisan's
pride in the Newhouse Law Center, I also see in this institution lessons of a more national scope. The exchange of perspectives, after all, the fruitful commingling of disparate
ideas, is a process that is dear to the First Amendment. This
Center brings together two institutions which, because of
their concern with this process, have the protection of the
First Amendment. The amendment extends a particular solic-
itude toward the "academic freedom" necessary for the conduct of a university; and the free operation of the press has
long been regarded as a bulwark of First Amendment liberties.

The productive cooperation of the press and the academy
illustrated by the creation of this Law Center is particularly
gratifying because it demonstrates so clearly the awareness of
a shared enterprise: without the informed citizenry that is the
product of a free press, the university would lack the informed audience necessary to receive and support its research; while without the education and scholarship offered
by the university, the press would lack the guidance, the informed perspective, so necessary for the meaningful reporting of events.

I must confess that I view this exemplary cooperation
with something approaching envy, for present attitudes of the
press toward the Supreme Court strongly suggest the complete absence of an enterprise shared by the press and the Supreme Court. Surely there is reason for that doubt when a respected and influential newspaper labels the Court's work of
last term "a virtual disaster," and others charge that the
Court has engaged in a "relentless assault" on the press, that
it is "dismantling" the First Amendment. The press, of
course, has in the past disagreed with rulings of the Court, but
I detect in the present controversy a new and disturbing note

of acrimony, almost bitterness. This is a serious and significant development, and worth a few moments reflection.

I begin with the premise that there exists a fundamental
and necessary interdependence of the Court and the press.
The press needs the Court, if only for the simple reason that
the Court is the ultimate guardian of the constitutional rights
that support the press. And the Court has a concomitant need
for the press, because through the press the Court receives
the tacit and accumulated experience of the nation, and—because the judgments of the Court ought also to instruct and to
inspire—the Court needs the medium of the press to fulfill
this task.

This partnership of the Court and the press is not unique;
it is merely exemplary of the function that the press serves in
our society. As money is to the economy, so the press is to our
political culture: it is the medium of circulation. It is the cur-
rency through which the knowledge of recent events is exchanged; the coin by which *public* discussion may be purchased.

This analogy, of course, cannot be pressed too far. Unlike
a medium of circulation, which receives the passive valuation
of others, the press is active, shaping and defining the very
arena in which events assume their public character. In this
the press performs a tripartite role. It chooses which events it
will publicize; it disseminates, to a greater or lesser extent,
selected information about these events; and it adopts toward
these events attitudes which are often instrumental in form-
ing public opinion.

These functions are of manifest importance for the political life of the nation. A democracy depends upon the existence of a *public* life and culture, and in a country of some
220 millions, this would scarcely be possible without the
press. I believe now, and have always believed, that, insofar
as the First Amendment shields the wellsprings of our democracy, it also provides protection for the press in the exercise of
these functions, for, as I said in an opinion for the Court many
years ago: the guarantees of the First Amendment "are not
for the benefit of the press so much as for the benefit of all of

us. A broadly defined freedom of the press assures the maintenance of our political system and an open society." [*Time,
Inc. vs Hill*]

In recent years the press has taken vigorous exception to
decisions of the Court circumscribing the protections the
First Amendment extends to the press in the exercise of these
functions. I have dissented from many of these opinions as
hampering, if not shackling the press' performance of its crucial role in helping maintain our open society, and have no
intention of standing here today to defend them. And I of
course fully support the right and duty of the press to express
its dissatisfaction with opinions of the Court with which it
disagrees. I am concerned, however, that in the heat of the
controversy the press may be misapprehending the fundamental issues at stake, and may consequently fail in its important task of illuminating these issues for the Court and the
public.

The violence of the controversy cannot be explained
merely by the fact that the Court has ruled adversely to the
press' interests. While the argument that the ability of the
press to function has suffered grievous and unjustified damage
may have merit in some cases, in others the vehemence of the
press' reaction has been out of all proportion to the injury
suffered. The source of the press' particular bitterness can, I
believe, be identified. It stems from the confusion of two distinct models of the role of the press in our society that claim
the protection of the First Amendment.

Under one model—which I call the "speech" model—the
press requires and is accorded the absolute protection of the
First Amendment. In the other model—I call it the "structural" model—the press' interests may conflict with other societal interests and adjustment of the conflict on occasion
favors the competing claim.

The "speech" model is familiar. It is as comfortable as a
pair of old shoes, and the press, in its present conflict with the
Court, most often slips into the language and rhetorical
stance with which this model is associated even when only
the "structural" model is at issue. According to this tradi-

tional "speech" model, the primary purpose of the First Amendment is more or less absolutely to prohibit any interference with freedom of expression. The press is seen as the public spokesman *par excellence*. Indeed, this model sometimes depicts the press as simply a collection of individuals who wish to speak out and broadly disseminate their views. This model draws its considerable power—I emphasize— from the abiding commitment we all feel to the right of self-expression, and, so far as it goes, this model commands the widest consensus. In the past two years, for example, the Court has twice unanimously struck down state statutes which prohibited the press from speaking out on certain subjects, and the Court has firmly rejected judicial attempts to muzzle press publication through prior restraints. The "speech" model thus readily lends itself to the heady rhetoric of absolutism.

The "speech" model, however, has its limitations. It is a mistake to suppose that the First Amendment protects *only* self-expression, only the right to speak out. I believe that the First Amendment in addition fosters the values of democratic self-government. In the words of Professor Zechariah Chafee, "[t]he First Amendment protects . . . a social interest in the attainment of truth, so that the country may not only adopt the wisest course of action but carry it out in the wisest way." [*Free Speech in the United States*] The amendment therefore also forbids the government from interfering with the communicative processes through which we citizens exercise and prepare to exercise our rights of self-government. The individual right to speak out, even millions of such rights aggregated together, will not sufficiently protect these social interests. It is in recognition of this fact that the Court has referred to "the circulation of information to which *the public is entitled* in virtue of the constitutional guarantees." [*Grosjean vs American Press Co.*]

Another way of saying this is that the First Amendment protects the structure of communications necessary for the existence of our democracy. This insight suggests the second model to describe the role of the press in our society. This second model is structural in nature. It focuses on the relationship of the press to the communicative functions required by our democratic beliefs. To the extent the press makes these functions possible, this model requires that it receive the protection of the First Amendment. A good example is the press' role in providing and circulating the information necessary for informed public discussion. To the extent the press, or, for that matter, to the extent that any institution uniquely performs this role, it should receive unique First Amendment protection.

This "structural" model of the press has several important implications. It significantly extends the umbrella of the press' constitutional protections. The press is not only shielded when it speaks out, but when it performs all the myriad tasks necessary for it to gather and disseminate the news. As you can easily see, the stretch of this protection is theoretically endless. Any imposition of any kind on the press will in some measure affect its ability to perform protected functions. Therefore this model requires a Court to weigh the effects of the imposition against the social interests which are served by the imposition. This inquiry is impersonal, almost sociological in nature. But it does not fit comfortably with the absolutist rhetoric associated with the first model of the press I have discussed. For here, I repeat, the Court must weigh the effects of the imposition inhibiting press access against the social interests served by the imposition.

The decisions that have aroused the sharpest controversy between the Court and the press have been those decisions in which the Court has tried to wrestle with the constitutional implications of this structural model of the press. For example, the reporters in *Branzburg vs Hayes* argued that if they were compelled to reveal confidential sources or notes before a Grand Jury, their ability to gather the news would be impaired. The case did not involve any substantive restrictions on press publications. The contention of the press was simply that reporters must be excused from duties imposed on all other citizens because the fulfillment of those duties would impair the press' ability to support the structure of communications protected by the First Amendment. In its decision, the Court acknowledged that First Amendment interests were involved in the process of news gathering, but concluded that these interests were outweighed by society's interest in the enforcement of the criminal law.

Similarly, in *Zurcher vs Stanford Daily,* a student newspaper contended that its offices could not be searched, as is usually the case, upon the issuance of a valid search warrant, but that a subpoena which would give the newspaper the opportunity to contest the search in advance was necessary. Again, the issue was not any restriction on what the newspaper could actually say, but rather whether special procedures were necessary to protect the press' ability to gather and publish the news. Once again, the Court held that whatever First Amendment interests were implicated were outweighed by society's interest in law enforcement.

Both these cases struck vehement, if not violent reactions from the press. About *Zurcher,* for example, the president of the American Newspaper Publishers Association stated that the opinion "puts a sledge hammer in the hands of those who would batter the American people's First Amendment rights." Unfortunately, the resulting controversy generated more heat than light, and the reason, I think, is that the press, in order to strengthen its rhetorical position, insisted on treating these cases exactly as if they involved only the traditional model of the press as public spokesman. The Washington *Star,* for example, argued that "it matters all too little whether abridgment takes the obvious forms of suppression and censorship, or the casual rummaging of a newspaper office on a search warrant." [6/3/78]

Of course, as I have been trying to make clear, it matters a great deal whether the press is abridged because restrictions are imposed on what it may say, or whether the press is abridged because its ability to gather the news or otherwise perform communicative functions necessary for a democracy is impaired. The two different situations stem from two distinct constitutional models of the press in our society, and require two distinct forms of analysis. The strong, absolutist rhetoric appropriate to the first model is only obfuscatory with respect to the second. The tendency of the press to confuse these two models has, in my opinion, been at the root of much of the recent acrimony in press-Court relations. The press has reacted as if its role as a public spokesman were being restricted, and, as a consequence, it has on occasion over-reacted.

Perhaps the clearest example is the recent case of *Herbert vs Lando*. The *Herbert* case was a lineal descendent of the decision of *New York Times Co. vs Sullivan. Sullivan* held that a public official could not successfully sue a media defendant for libel unless he could demonstrate that the alleged defamatory publication was issued with "actual malice," that is with knowing or reckless disregard of the truth. Subsequent decisions extended this holding to public figures, like Colonel Herbert, and made clear that actual malice turned on the media defendant's "subjective awareness of probable falsity." [*Gertz vs Robert Welch, Inc.*] The theory of *Sullivan* was that if the media were liable for large damage judgments for the publication of false defamatory information, the resulting inhibitions might undermine the robust public discussion so essential to a democracy. If a journalist knew that he was publishing defamatory falsehood, however, the First Amendment would offer him no protection.

The *Herbert* case raised the question whether a public-figure plaintiff could in discovery ask a defendant journalist about his state of mind when publishing the alleged defamatory falsehood. Now it is clear that a journalist's state of mind is relevant to his "subjective awareness of probable falsity," and thus to the issue of actual malice. And traditionally a plaintiff is entitled to discovery on all relevant issues. Privileges are rare and strictly construed. Nevertheless, the press argued that it could not perform its functions under the First Amendment unless a special "editorial" privilege were created to shield it from such inquiries.

The Court rejected this argument, and the result was a virtually unprecedented outpouring of scathing criticism. See Marquis Childs, The CBS Case: Reasons for Resentment,

Washington *Post* [5/1/79]. The decision was labeled "judicial Agnewism" [Washington *Star*, 4/20/79] and a "legal nightmare." [The Birmingham *News*, 4/19/79] One paper said that the decision was an example of the Court following "its anti-press course into what can only be called an Orwellian domain," [The Miami *Herald*, 4/20/79] while the managing editor of the St. Louis *Post-Dispatch* stated that the opinion "has the potential of totally inhibiting the press to a degree seldom seen outside a dictatorial or fascist country." [The Birmingham *News*, 4/19/79]

I dissented in part in *Herbert*, but I can say with some degree of confidence that the decision deserved a more considered response on the part of the press than it received. The injury done the press was simply not of the magnitude to justify the resulting firestorm of acrimonious criticism. In its rush to cudgel the Court, the press acted as if the decision imposed restrictions on what the press could say, as though the actual malice standard of *Sullivan* were overruled. In fact two newspapers actually erroneously characterized the opinion as holding that truth would no longer be an absolute defense to libel suits, [the *Times-Pacayune* (New Orleans), the Birmingham *News*] while several others appeared to read the opinion as reverting to the old common-law definition of "malice" as ill will. [NY *Times*, the *Star Ledger*, the *Atlanta Constitution*, the *Oregonian*] Putting aside, however, such unfortunate examples of inaccurate reporting the deepest source of the press' outrage was I think well captured by William Leonard, president of CBS news. Mr. Leonard said that *Herbert* denied constitutional protection to "the journalist's most precious possession—his mind, his thoughts and his editorial judgment." [N. Y. *Times*, 4/19/79]

I understand and sympathize with Mr. Leonard's concern. Being asked about one's state of mind can be a demeaning and unpleasant experience. Nevertheless, the inquiry into a defendant's state of mind, into his intent, is one of the most common procedures in the law. Almost all crimes require that some element of the defendant's intent be established, as do all intentional torts, such as trespass, assault, or conversion.

State of mind can also be relevant to questions of fraud, mistake, and recklessness. And, in the area of libel, it would scarcely be fair to say that a plaintiff can only recover if he establishes intentional falsehood and at the same time to say that he cannot inquire into a defendant's intentions.

But in its outrage against the *Herbert* decision, the press unfortunately misapprehended the role model of the press involved. To it the decision was simply a "George Orwellian invasion of the mind," [Los Angeles *Times,* 4/19/79] which meant, as Jack Landau, director of the Reporters Committee for Freedom of the Press put it, that "the press will soon have lost the last constitutional shred of its editorial privacy and independence from the government." [the *Times-Picayune,* 4/20/79] The true role model involved can be ignored, however, only on the assumption that a journalist's state of mind is somehow special, and cannot be impinged for any purpose. It is important to note that this assumption gathers its rhetorical basis from the model of the press as public spokesman. For when a citizen speaks publically he *is* special, and, with only rare and stringent exceptions, what he says cannot be restricted for any purpose. But, as I have made clear, this is not the model of the press at issue in *Herbert.* The decision does not affect the actual malice standard set out in *Sullivan.* Instead the question raised by *Herbert* is whether the press' ability to perform the communicative functions required by our democratic society would be significantly impaired if an editorial privilege were not created.

Note that this is a difficult and factual question, and one that cannot be illuminated by sharp or sensational rhetoric. In my view reporters will not cease to publish because they are later asked about their state of mind. On the other hand, predecisional communications among editors may well be curtailed if they may later be used as evidence in libel suits. Since a democracy requires an informed and accurate press, and since predecisional editorial communications contribute to informed and accurate editorial judgments, I would have held that such communications should receive a qualified privilege. I say a *qualified* privilege because even the execu-

tive privilege bestowed upon the President of the United
States so that he may receive the informed and unimpeded
advice of his aides is, as the case of *United States vs Nixon*
makes clear, a qualified privilege.

A majority of my colleagues rejected my position because
it believed that the accuracy of resulting publications would
not be impaired if predecisional editorial communications
were revealed. This is a matter of judgment, about which
reasonable men may differ. It is also, at least in form, an empirical question, upon which the lessons of later experience
may be persuasively brought to bear. If the press wishes to
play a part in this process, it must carefully distinguish the
basis on which its constitutional claim is based, and it must
tailor its arguments and its rhetoric accordingly. This may involve a certain loss of innocence, a certain recognition that
the press, like other institutions, must accommodate a variety
of important social interests. But the sad complexity of our
society makes this inevitable, and there is no alternative but a
shrill and impotent isolation.

These are hard words, but there is much at stake, not the
least of which is the ability of the press to resume its sure
voice as a reliable conscience of this nation. Last term there
were decisions of the Supreme Court justifying far more concern than *Herbert vs Lando* and about which the press was
uniquely qualified to speak. Yet the credibility of the press
was impaired by the excesses of its reactions to *Lando*. An example is the case of *Gannett Co., Inc. vs DePasquale*, in
which the Court, in a 5–4 vote, held that members of the
public had no constitutional right under the Sixth and Four-
teenth Amendments to attend pretrial hearings in a criminal
case.

Gannett involves the Sixth rather than the First Amendment and so does not fit into either of the two models I have
sketched out. The case concerns the right of the public, not
merely of the press, and at its heart is interpretation of the
kind of government we have set for ourselves in our Constitution. The question is whether that government will be visible
to the people, who are its authors. *Gannett* holds that judges,

as officers of that government, may in certain circumstances remove themselves from public view and perhaps also holds that they can make this decision without even considering the interests of the people. I believe that the Framers did not conceive such a government, and that they had in mind the truth precisely captured several generations later by Lord Acton: "Everything secret degenerates, even the administration of justice."

Any damage by the Court's decision in *Gannett* can of course be undone through legislative enactments, should a concerned citizenry so demand. The clear voice of the press, however, is an essential part of any such enterprise, especially about a subject that bears so closely on press' business. The press did, I am happy to note, intelligently and searchingly criticize the *Gannett* decision. It was distinctly noted that the decision was "much more than another controversial 'press case,' " but was in fact "a decision about the relationship of the public to the judicial process." [NY *Times*, 7/4/79] The point I wish to stress, however, is that the impact of the press' quite correct reaction was undercut by the unjustified violence of its previous responses to *Herbert vs. Lando* and other such cases involving the structural model of the press. This fact was cogently noted by Anthony Lewis in his column in the New York *Times* [7/5/79]:

> The press ... should forswear absolutes. The reiterated claim of recent years that its freedom has no limits has done the press no good. If the press began recognizing that these are difficult issues, involving more than one interest, it could more effectively criticize the facile simplicities of a Gannett decision.

I think Mr. Lewis is correct. And I say this with some urgency, for the integrity of the press must be preserved, not only for cases like *Gannett*, where the press puts forward the claims of the public, but even for cases like *Zurcher*, where the press puts forward its own structural claims. For the application of the First Amendment is far from certain in the as yet uncharted domains foreshadowed by the structural model of the press. The Court needs help in scouting these dim areas in which the shield of the Amendment is put forward not to guard the personal right to speak, but to protect social functions of impersonal dimensions. The press can and must assist the Court in mustering proper legal conclusions from the accumulated experience of the nation. But the press can be of assistance only if bitterness does not cloud its vision, nor self-righteousness its judgment.

The dedication of the Samuel I. Newhouse Law Center, however, is an occasion for hope. The Center stands as a symbol of conciliation between the press and the law. It gives one reason to trust that the shared enterprise of the press and the Court will once again resume, even if it is to be expressed through the traditional form of healthy and productive disagreement.

SCIENCE AND TECHNOLOGY

NEW POLICY OPTIONS THROUGH TECHNOLOGY[1]

HARRISON SCHMITT [2]

On March 19, 1980, Harrison Schmitt, Republican senator from New Mexico, gave the keynote address at the first Technology Exchange Conference and Exposition, at the new convention center in Baltimore, Maryland, for state and local officials in the mid-Atlantic region. The meeting was co-sponsored by Senator Charles McC. Mathias Jr. of Maryland (Republican) and the Federal Laboratory Consortium for Technology Transfer.

Because of his unique background, Senator Schmitt is much in demand as a speaker on space subjects. After earning a doctorate in geology at Harvard in 1964, he joined the NASA Apollo program and became a lunar module pilot and geologist on Apollo 17, landing on the moon in 1972. After serving as NASA Assistant Administrator for Energy Programs in 1974–75, he resigned and returned to his home state of New Mexico, where he was elected to the US Senate in 1976.

In his brief talk, he outlines the new policy options declaring that "technology . . . will be the basic ingredient of successful national policy." In the spirit of the space age he envisions "a second Solar System Exploration" in the 21st century and a "permanent settlement on Mars." Not long ago, such suggestions would have only been considered material for science fiction, but they are now given credence by a US senator and a former astronaut.

Throughout its history, science and technology have provided the United States with its most significant new national policy options. The overwhelming majority of the American people and the people of the world believe this to be true and will be true in the future. Look at a few of the more obvious examples from the past:

The Transcontinental railroad opened up a continent and preserved the destiny of a new nation.

---

[1] Delivered at the first Technology Exchange Conference and Exposition, Convention Center, Baltimore, Maryland, March 19, 1980. Quoted by permission.
[2] For biographical note, see Appendix.

The automation of manufacturing laid the foundation for our early economy and the defense of freedom in two world wars.

The on-going agricultural revolution not only has fed our people and spurred their economic growth, but has fed much of the world.

The science and technology of oil and gas exploration provided the base for our modern national growth.

The construction of the Panama Canal established the US as the dominant maritime and trading nation of the world as well as created new technology for our industry.

The harnessing of nuclear energy, although incomplete, ended a war, prevented other wars, and could provide inexhaustible energy for mankind if we are wise enough to handle it.

The electronics revolution has drawn the people of the world together with a potential for good unmatched in history.

The vast base of technology from our space endeavors supplies a continuous stream of new services in an infinite number of areas including health care, communications, computers, energy efficiency, consumer products, and environmental protection.

There are many more examples which, on close examination, show that new policy options were created by science and technology for the expansion, growth and protection of the nation and the vast improvement of the well-being of its citizens. True, through ignorance or neglect there have been adverse consequences from these new technologies, but the total benefits far outweigh the costs. Few Americans would advocate turning back the clock; however, as we move even more aggressively into the future, we must learn from the mistakes in judgment in the past.

Four areas of new science and technology which illustrate the significance of the policy options potentially available to the nation are basic biological research, laser technology, information systems, and space technologies.

First, basic biological research is opening windows to vistas of preventative medicine never before imagined. As in the 1930s, when the accumulation of a century of medical observations made possible the successful treatment and cure of many diseases through antibiotics, now fundamental understanding of biological and biochemical processes is making possible the prevention of many diseases.

The prevention of disease must be the ultimate goal we can imagine for medical science. The understanding of genes and how they work or don't work; the understanding of chemical and electrical communications within the body; the understanding of the effects and workings of carcinogenic substances, including viruses; and the understanding of the most intimate functioning of the cardiovascular system are just a few of the scientific breakthroughs that are in progress. The potential of such breakthroughs are unlimited when combined with the capabilities of the new technologies of recombinant DNA, electromagnetic sensing, synthetic biochemical production, artificial microelectronic biosystems, computerized axial tomographic (CAT) scanners, ultrasonic scanners, computer processing, and many other marvels of the age.

Already, we can foresee the availability of large quantities of preventive medicines such as insulin produced by recombinant DNA technology; of neurological diagnosis that prevents or cures nerve and mental disorders; of numerous prostoglandins which promise therapy for ailments ranging from arthritis to glaucoma, from ulcers to asthma, from high blood pressure to migraine headaches; of artificial organs and body chemicals including the heart and blood; of 100 percent cure rates for certain types of cancer; and of the ultimate prediction of the susceptability to disease and thus its avoidance.

Basic biochemical research is opening up the new option of disease prevention rather than costly treatment and is the eventual alternative to ever rising medical bills and unaffordable insurance.

Second, laser technology is providing spectacular options for chemical processing and national defense. On the one hand, lasers that can be turned to the characteristic vibrations of elements and isotopics make possible both the efficient separation of useful materials from waste and the destruction of harmful chemical compounds before they enter man's environment.

An obvious application of laser chemical separation is in the management of nuclear wastes. Such wastes can become resources available at low cost and low risk while at the same time helping to re-open the nuclear power energy option for the country.

Laser chemical destruction is equally valuable in the cleanup of toxic chemicals before their possible introduction into the environment. Again, at low cost and low risk, technologies that could otherwise harm the environment can become servants of our economy.

Laser technology also opens up the possibility of shifting the emphasis of our strategic defense policy from one of "massive retaliation" or "mutually assured destruction" to a policy of mutually assured protection. High power ground or space-based laser systems, properly integrated with detection, communication and control systems, may permit the surgical destruction of attacking missiles before there is a need to consider retaliation.

Mutually assured protection, as a concept for national defense policy, cannot be fully implemented overnight or even for several years. However, through technology, the transition to this policy must begin if mankind is to have any long-term hope for avoiding war and perpetuating freedom.

Third, information systems technology, in the broadest sense, makes it possible to rationally imagine the gradual elimination of hunger, disease, poverty, and ignorance in the underdeveloped portions of the world. These four horsemen of disaster are rushing down on mankind and freedom at unparalleled speeds. However, for the first time in human history, we can consider technically realistic means of stopping their onslaught and using that capability as the foundation of our foreign policy toward the underdeveloped nations of the world.

The foundations for this new foreign policy lie in the gathering, analysis, distribution, and use of information. The decade of the '80s can become the age of information.

The collection and distribution of information on a worldwide basis via satellite has provided a distinct change in the course of human history. The most graphic demonstration of this change came when, on Christmas Eve, 1968, hundreds of millions of human beings throughout the world, simultaneously had a new thought about a familiar object in the night sky—the Moon. The men of Apollo 8 were there, and the Moon would never be the same for anyone. Now, we realize that the world will never be the same; that there are solutions to those age-old problems of the human condition on Earth. There are solutions if we are wise enough to reach out and grasp them.

Through technology, we can and should create programs aimed at permanent, eventually self-financing, services for worldwide communications, weather and ocean forecasting, earth resources discovery or monitoring, societal services, and prediction of natural events of disastrous human consequences or broad scale economic impact.

Through technology we can and should help underdeveloped nations create agricultural, health, resource, and educational systems that permit their entry into the 20th century.

It is know-how they need, not just physical assistance.

Finally, space technologies in general provide the foundation for the movement of our civilization of freedom into space. The space policy for the decades of the '80s and '90s should provide for the creation of the permanent facilities of our civilization in space, reorganizing our historically inevitable competition there, as well as on Earth, with the Soviet-dominated civilization of oppression.

These Earth orbit facilities will utilize and augment this unique research, service, and manufacturing environment.

The weightlessness, the vacuum, the unique view of the Earth, sun and stars provide unparalleled opportunities for research, education, space power production, manufacturing, health care, and even recreational activities.

Permanent facilities in orbit will provide capabilities that relate directly to current and growing problems facing this nation. For example, the creation of new export commodities and services and the supply of inexhaustible energy are needs that cannot be ignored by this generation, nor denied to future generations. In addition, the now real possibility of research, education, health care, and recreation in space has caught the imagination of millions of young Americans. Let us not disappoint them, or the future.

In the first decade of the 21st century, a space policy for our civilization should initiate a second Solar System Exploration decade. This is the time about which most of the very young have their dreams. Bases and settlements on the Moon, missions of exploration to Mars and Venus, and the beginnings of the establishment of a Martian settlement, all are the stuff these dreams are made of. The parents of the first Martians are looking over our shoulder as they work and dream their way through elementary school, high school, and college.

It is the idea of a permanent settlement on Mars that seems most intriguing to the young people of today. They can visualize taking part in this next great expansion of the human race and its civilization and the ingredients for self-sustaining settlements on Mars appear to already exist.

There are a few technical hurdles between us and settlements on Mars, compared to those which faced us when we began our race to the moon. This technological option is ours for the taking. Now, the challenge is to develop the national motivation to proceed.

Ladies and gentlemen, technology has been and will be the basic ingredient of successful national policies of the past, present, and future. To ignore this fact would be to ignore our strength as a nation and our formula for survival.

SCIENCE AND THE PUBLIC TRUST[1]

JOHN W. WYDLER[2]

On March 28, 1979, the United States suffered its first nuclear accident at Three Mile Island in the Susquehanna River near Middletown, Pennsylvania. The reaction to it approached hysteria in nearby communities. Immediately afterward, public support for further nuclear power development declined from 69 percent to 46 percent (NY *Times*—CBS News Poll, Ap. 10, '79), and the Nuclear Regulatory Commission (NRC) ordered the closure of all similar reactors. Throughout the country, opposition to further nuclear development mounted, and many existing facilities (total in the US are 71 and generate about 13.5 percent of the electricity) were picketed. During the first three months of 1980, plans for ten nuclear plants were cancelled or deferred, regulations are in a muddle, and the NRC continues to restrict licensing. In spite of the public fears that the Three Mile Island accident engendered, power executives, public officials, and some scientists continue to insist that nuclear power is the only way the United States can meet its power needs in the mid-nineteen eighties.

Disturbed by adverse reaction to the accident and nuclear technology in general, John W. Wydler, US Representative from New York, spoke at 8:15 P.M. on October 18, 1979, at the Empire State Plaza to about 200 corporate associates of the American Institute of Physics (Schenectady, NY). Describing himself as "a layman without extensive scientific training," he was modest about his considerable knowledge. He is a booster of nuclear energy and as ranking minority member of the Science and Technology and the Energy Research and Development sub-committees in the House of Representatives, he has had the opportunity to learn the facts and study public reaction.

In his introduction, he got right to the point by stating clearly what he intended to ask of his audience. Arguing that the public is uninformed about environmental effects of nuclear technology, he told his audience that it is their "responsibility—and opportunity . . . to play an important role" in the form of industrial lectures. He declared that "breakdowns of public trust adversely affect na-

---

[1] Delivered to the corporate associate group of the American Institute of Physics in Schenectady, New York, 8:15 P.M., October 18, 1979. Quoted by permission.
[2] For biographical note, see Appendix.

tional energy policy" and scientific progress. Public misconceptions about risk and mistrust of technologists, not scientists, combine to defeat worthwhile projects, those steps toward solving our energy crisis.

I speak to you tonight as a layman without extensive scientific training and I speak to you as a legislator that knows he needs your help. More important—the country needs your help. One of the most controversial aspects of our national energy policy revolves around the question of public trust. Public pressure results in political decisions that often ignore the scientific fact because the public is uninformed or misinformed. The public must be informed and it is your responsibility—and opportunity—to play an important role.

The question of public trust is dramatized, and the public's sensitivity to such issues is heightened, when technology moves from the research laboratory into the arena of demonstration, development, and operation. A good example is the public reaction to the recent Three Mile Island nuclear accident. Public confidence in the nuclear physicist was not at all affected. But many of the people interviewed since TMI have indicated reservations about nuclear engineering.

The environmental effects of a technology do not become controversial until the government or industry is ready to demonstrate and utilize the technology. The Clinch River Breeder Reactor is striking proof of this fact. As long as the breeder concept was explored on a small scale, and on an experimental basis the environmentalists did not show great concern. But, when government and industry proposed to build a breeder plant which would actually generate 375 megawatts of electrical power, then the "hue and cry" resounded from the no-growth camp.

Such breakdowns of public trust adversely affect the formulation of national energy policy. The public perception of advanced technology must be improved to develop the public trust that will permit technology demonstration, without which all research is an academic exercise.

Strong national leadership and responsible public education are key requirements for maintaining public trust in science and technology. Without them, the citizenry can be subjected to scare stories with no foundation in reality. Such distortions misinform the public and distort the facts about the country's technological choices.

The broader question, of course, is whether this country will continue, as some perceptive technologists have recently noted, "to believe that science and technology have continually pushed the limitations of man's ability to live in the circumstances provided by nature" and that "there arts can continue to do so." Sustaining this belief will require public education to dispel current apprehensions about perceived negative impacts of science and technology.

In other words, how well we handle the public trust question in energy may determine our prospects for reaping future fruits from promising advanced technologies. Without public acceptance, technology will wither—and science will suffer. Whether we advocate nuclear fission or magnetic fusion power, we are all in this together. We are squared off against people who feel that any central power generation is morally wrong.

Let me cite a major instance of national energy policy where—based on gross misperceptions of real risks—the administration decided to forsake advanced technology. They made this unfortunate choice chiefly on a visceral basis without any real comparative study. And in doing so, they contributed to the huge gap between perception and reality.

Just as technology historically has enabled man to tap increasingly large resources, the breeder reactor provides an avenue to a virtually limitless energy using natural uranium. However, the present administration has steadfastly refused to make a commitment to demonstrate breeder reactor technology as a reasonable insurance policy on our energy future. It talks "solar" and "conservation" because they are sugar-coated words without adverse public reaction.

"Perceived risk" was cited as a major factor in the President's position on the Breeder. He began with a stated concern about the proliferation aspects of breeder technology and reprocessing. Although he has since given other reasons for killing the Clinch River Project, the President's rationale was first adopted in response to strong environmental pressures. His view is based on the assumption that the international community cannot arrive at a combination of proper technical fixes and collective safeguard agreements to minimize proliferation risks even within several decades.

In the near-term nuclear arena, the recent Three Mile Island accident is now serving as a reason for delaying rapid deployment of light water reactors. Certainly public perception of the consequences of a catastrophic nuclear accident calls for enhanced safety measures. Unfortunately, there is a climate of mistrust surrounding the nuclear industry since the early days of government involvement and this public perception has recently been exploited by nuclear opponents. The distorted picture which is displayed to the public may even have reduced the chances of using the accident results in a positive way so that nuclear safety can be improved.

We have heard calls for a nuclear moratorium in various states, including our great State of New York, based on the same unreasoned fear which the anti-nuclear zealots have shown and the administration has reinforced. In addition to safety, the anti-nuclear critics have continued to use the nuclear waste management issue with great effectiveness. The administration again has compounded the felony by refusing to state reasonable goals for terminal isolation of nuclear waste.

Anti-nuclear governors have seized upon this indecisiveness as a major reason for foreclosing the nuclear option. And yet the overwhelming facts are that in disposing of nuclear waste we have nothing to fear but fear itself.

It has become clear to us on the Committee on Science and Technology that a combination of sound waste treatment technology and careful geology can achieve reasonable terminal isolation goals. The administration's mishandled study by the Interagency Review Group on waste management not only failed to stress the past federal experience in handling nuclear waste, but also left ambiguous the question of what really constitutes adequate isolation of nuclear waste. The average man thinks the problem is insoluble, while Edward Teller describes it as a non-problem.

The man in the street can hardly feel confident about the

nuclear option when officials at the highest levels of government have provided such a warped and cloudy view of the real risks of the technology, and the President seems afraid to mention the word nuclear.

A classic case where we are just beginning to see efforts to kill a technology by creating public distrust is magnetic fusion energy. The Union of Concerned Scientists recently showed us "the tip of the iceberg" when they voiced concern about tritium as a fuel for fusion reactors.

I have been warning the fusion community for the past two years to expect increasing environmental "flak" as this concept moves into the technology development phase. I predict that, once it is announced that a fusion plant is to be built to demonstrate the technology in an integrated fashion and to generate electricity, then the attack will begin in dead earnest. It happened to Clinch River. It will happen to magnetic fusion. And I even predict it will happen to solar energy if and when it really becomes productive. Already attacks on the Solar Satellite are heard in Congress on environmental grounds.

The public will be told that tritium is the most sinister substance known to man—even more sinister than that devilish substance plutonium—and that fusion also raises proliferation concerns. The environmentalists will stress the technical possibility of a fission/fusion hybrid machine and the prodigious amounts of plutonium such a device would be capable of generating.

So will go the attack.

My warning is simple: the fusion community must begin now to counter all of these criticisms and emphasize the inherent safety of their reactors so that the public develops substantial trust in the concept. Some of the breeder reactor controversy could have been avoided if that sector of the fission community had laid more extensive ground work in informing the public on real and perceived proliferation concerns.

Realistically, of course, the approach taken in educating the public on these topics can slant public perception one way or another. The desire to sensationalize will always be present and we must assume that the real story will be distorted. Thus, we must utilize the devil's advocacy approach to work out rational counterpoints early in the game.

The most important ingredient to public trust in science and technology is the public perception of the scientist or technologist. Also, we must realize that, although the citizenry may hold the scientist in high regard, the technologist will undoubtedly come under suspicion whenever it appears that developed technology will affect the citizen in an adverse way. This may involve overlooking the obvious benefits of technology and focusing on its perceived environmental impacts or on safety concerns surrounding its use.

The bottom line is that strong leadership and responsible information which give the people the facts are absolute requirements if the public is to retain trust in science and technology. Public education must not be based on perceived risks which are misinterpreted by the extremists, but must be founded on the real technological risks derived from systematic comparisons of alternatives.

We have seen an extreme perception gap in nuclear power and the administration is allowing it to grow. It would be fair to say the government should lead, but it will not. Politics will ensure a split voice or forked tongue—the media will stress the negative, and the decision will hang in the balance.

The public still trusts the scientists and that, for you, is both a burden and an opportunity. You must fill the perception gap with responsible public education because the citizenry will look to you for the facts.

Every scientist involved in the future of energy has a common stake in this battle for the minds of our citizens.

It will be little comfort if the fusion program grows, while the breeder program is killed. That would simply make fusion the next battleground. Science is merely a means to an end. The scientific community must mobilize its forces to educate the public.

As a nation, we must continue to believe that complex technology can be controlled and we must go forward with its development. Otherwise, technology will be curtailed all the way back to the laboratory bench.

I have been informed of both your visiting scientist program and the American Physical Society's visiting physicist program to provide hands-on experience to university scientists in an industrial environment. These are positive, proper activities for your organizations and I commend you.

It seems to me, however, that you must do more. A program intended to provide industrial lecturers to present the real costs and benefits of energy technology would be a natural extension of your existing programs. It would be logical for you, the AIP Corporate Associates, to sponsor such an information program. The AIP would make the decisions on lecturers and schedules and could provide a list of available lecturers and suggested topics to universities.

This would be a supplement to your existing programs. But just as important, as individuals and in your corporate capacities, you must expand your efforts in carrying the message to the American people. As scientists, you can present the facts about energy technologies.

You must insist that the technologies be compared on an objective basis. You must use every reasonable mechanism of public education to push for reasonable choices.

Public education is your duty. Don't shrink from it. The future of America's technology and progress is at stake.

ENVIRONMENTAL REGULATION AND THE IMMOBILIZATION OF TRUTH[1]

Gus Speth[2]

Public concern about how to protect the planet earth from the ravages of man is growing. Toxic seepage in Love Canal in Niagara Falls, New York, and other comparable incidents have blazed in headlines lately. How can the nation protect its air, wild life, soil, other natural resources, and living space? Who should foot the

[1] Delivered at the Fifth National Conference on the Environmental Industry Council, L'Enfant Plaza Hotel, February 28, 1980. Quoted by permission.
[2] For biographical note, see Appendix.

bill? Is it the responsibility of private enterprise or is it a responsibility of the government? Gus Speth, chairman of the President's
Council of Environmental Quality attempted to answer these
questions at the Fifth National Conference of the Environmental
Industry Council meeting at the L'Enfant Plaza Hotel, Washington, D.C. on February 23, 1980.

In his speech, he lists the many pieces of environmental legislation and environmental accomplishments of this administration.
He also refutes arguments by business against government regulations and red tape, by pointing out a number of instances where
business would not think of giving up regulations designed to protect them in many areas.

This speech presents another facet of the subject discussed in
the previous speech by Representative John W. Wydler, namely
the nuclear power controversy. Wydler mentioned "enhanced
safety measures." Mr. Speth goes into more detail on what measures the government is taking and how they have been received
by the public and by business.

I want to congratulate you on this Fifth National Conference of the Environmental Industry Council.

Not only are we here to mark five years of cooperation,
we are also at the conjunction of a series of important anni-
versaries and events: the tenth anniversary of both Earth Day
and the signing of the National Environmental Policy Act,
and, of course, the Second Environmental Decade ceremony
tomorrow at the White House.

Historian and Congressional Librarian Daniel Boorstin
makes a distinction between an event and what he calls a
"pseudoevent." An event, obviously, is an important or at
least memorable occurrence that can range upward on the
vertical scale from Neil Armstrong's first footprint on the
moon downward to the sinking of the Titanic.

A pseudoevent is subsequently celebrating an event.

To the extent that pseudoevents are nothing but public
relations exercises promoting the forgettable, they are as superfluous as watching the Pittsburgh Steelers play the San
Francisco Forty-Niners.

But by no means all pseudoevents *are* superfluous. Our
national and religious holidays are not superfluous. Anniver-

saries of significant achievements, whether they involve a closer look at the moon or a better look at our earth, must be remembered, recalled, and reinforced, or we are in danger of losing our heritage, neglecting constructive pride in past achievement, and failing to exploit legitimate opportunities to gain a better perspective on where we are, how far we have come—or regressed—and what we must do.

Today, I want to explore where we are, how far we have come, and what we must do after ten years under NEPA. I want to do so with particular reference to Federal environmental regulation—its past and future.

From an environmental perspective, the past decade reflects the American people and their system of government at their very finest. Faced with the increasingly likely prospect of leaving their children a legacy of silent springs, the American people called for action, and their government responded with imagination and creativity.

In a single sustained burst of legislation, almost without precedent in our history, machinery to reverse a century of environmental degradation was devised, perfected, and set into motion. NEPA, signed on the first day of the last decade, was quickly followed by important amendments to the Clean Air Act, the Occupational Safety and Health Act, the Resources Recovery Act, and establishment of the EPA [Environmental Protection Agency]. Building on this foundation, Congress rapidly added the Federal Water Pollution Control Act, the Ocean Dumping Act, the Safe Drinking Water Act, a strengthened Federal Insecticide, Fungicide and Rodenticide Act, the Toxic Substances Control Act, the Resource Conservation and Recovery Act, the Noise Control Act, and the Quiet Communities Act.

I have no doubt whatsoever that future generations of Americans will look back upon this decade of environmental renaissance the way we look back upon similar creative bursts of legislation during the 1930s, for the New Deal, and 1960s for civil rights: as among democracy's finest hours.

And there are other positive dimensions that must be cited.

I think it is very important that we have continued to make progress in the past few years, when energy and economic issues have competed mightily for public attention.

Despite these pressures, we have maintained the commitment to a clean, healthy environment for all of our citizens, and the administration's legislative program now before Congress—which includes such vital measures as the Alaska Lands Bill, the "superfund" bill to pay for the cleanup of abandoned hazardous waste sites, a new plan for nuclear waste management, proposals to increase funding for energy conservation and the development of solar and other renewable energy sources, and reform of federal water resource development—indicates a continuing environmental priority. It is important that Congress move forward with these measures.

Another positive dimension involves the actions of individuals and thousands of private groups and businesses which have contributed so greatly to protecting the environment. Much of the progress we have made so far would not have been possible without a strong pollution control industry, and I congratulate you and your association for the role you have played.

But even as we rejoice in these positive dimensions, our celebration is shadowed to some degree by contrary evidence.

One of the negative dimensions we face is psychological. It stems from the fact that too often some of us exhibit a truncated attention span. Causes, ideas, attitudes have, it appears, a short half-life, with today's compelling cause tarnished into tomorrow's discarded fashion.

Those who argue against continuing the environmental momentum of the 1970s have failed to grasp the full severity and dimensions of the environmental problems that continue to face us. The issues that persist today are not just questions of esthetics, or comfort, or an idealized notion of "the good life"; they are clear threats to the health and welfare of the American people. They simply cannot be put aside until a time when it is more convenient to focus on them.

We have gained success in combatting gross threats to our

air and water only to discover whole new phalanxes of subtle menaces, whose danger and obstinacy often vary in inverse proportion to their ability to be quickly and easily understood. Thus, we look upon the clarifying water and purified air with satisfaction while, stealthily, four square miles of our most productive farm land are each day consumed by concrete and asphalt and lost from agriculture. Fish are returning to waters they long ago fled, but we are finding their flesh often contains significant amounts of toxic chemicals. Sulfur dioxide pollution is now a major health problem in only a few areas, but partly because we are airmailing sulfur oxides to places far away where it falls as acid rain.

There are few who directly attack our environmental commitment, but a growing number have adopted the strategy of undermining that commitment indirectly. At first the strategy took the form of a refreshing concern for the working man and woman. In a kind of perversion of the Phillips curve once vainly used to explain inflation, the argument seemed to run that unemployment went up as smog and oil slicks went down. But that argument was permitted to die a quiet death when the National Academy of Sciences estimated that the nation's effort to clean up the environment actually accounted for about 680,000 jobs, 30 new jobs for every one eliminated due to decisions by manufacturing firms and others that resulted from environmental requirements. A subsequent study by Data Resources, Inc. showed that air and water pollution controls will stimulate employment during the entire 16-year period from 1970 to 1986.

The negative strategy then moved to the issue of inflation. This has now been looked into as well, and it has been found that between 1979 and 1986, federal environmental regulations will add between one- and two-tenths of one percentage point to the annual inflation rate. For 1980, existing federal environmental regulation is predicted to add only one tenth of a percentage point to the rate at which prices increase—a rate that should continue in the period 1984 to 1986.

The first point to note is that, even by standard economic measures, the inflationary impact of environmental programs is quite minor. Moreover, any realistic modification of federal environmental regulations would produce no significant reduction in the overall Consumer Price Index. If the inflationary impact of these requirements could be reduced by a fourth—a substantial relaxation—the CPI's increase would be restrained by less than 0.05 percent: the net effect of even draconian measures could be the difference between a 7 percent and 7.05 percent increase in the CPI. So we must look elsewhere than environmental regulations for the sources of inflation, and for the proper targets of our anti-inflation efforts.

Following the bankruptcy of these contentions, we have been told and told, and then told again, that environmental regulation is merely one aspect of an already over-regulated society, a society forced to divert increasingly scarce resources and managerial talent from productive and innovative ends. Indeed, some major corporations have undertaken rather large campaigns to convince the American people that government regulation is out of control.

In response, I would simply point out that, in light of the continuing revelations of corporate neglect or worse, much of the current protestation against government regulation rings awfully hollow. Virtually every environmental regulation, for example, has its genesis in some problem, like Love Canal or Kepone or PCB's, that threatened the public and finally brought a legitimate public demand for government action. Regulation is not going to go away until the problems do. The way we regulate can *and must* be improved, but let us face the fact that a continued high level of government regulatory activity is *essential* to national goals of paramount importance—to controlling cancer and protecting health, to preventing consumer fraud and deception, to cleaning up air and water pollution, to reducing oil imports and conserving energy, to protecting us from improperly sited or mismanaged nuclear power facilities—the list, obviously, is very long.

Some critics of government regulation do rely on factual presentations, rather than rhetorical overkill, to make their case. For example, Clifford P. Hardin, former Agriculture Secretary and now Vice Chairman of the board of Ralston Purina Company, put it this way:

... my concern, and that of most people who share my concern, is not with the idea of regulation, or even with the central purpose of most regulatory legislation. Some regulation is a must and most of us support it. Our concern is rather with such things as overlapping and duplication in requests for information often in different formats; directly conflicting rules from separate agencies; rules that are out of date, but which are not removed; and, finally and perhaps most importantly, the growing obsession with minutia— items that have little, if anything to do with protecting the consumer, environment, the safety and welfare of employees, or the growth of competitors.

I could not agree more, and this administration could not agree more, with Mr. Hardin's sentiments. No function of government, and that definitely includes the regulatory function, should be transformed into a kind of sacred cow, immune from critical examination.

And that is precisely why President Carter is, as one of the central initiatives of his administration, reaffirmed in his most recent State of the Union Address, determined to eliminate the kinds of problems referred to by Mr. Hardin.

Thus, among other steps, President Carter has ordered regulatory agencies:

.... to analyze the costs and benefits of major proposed regulations, to assure that alternative approaches are articulated, consequences compared and the rationale for decisions elaborated, and good reasons provided if the least expensive option is not chosen;
.... to make sure that top officials supervise the regulation-writing process;
.... to review existing regulations regularly in order to weed out those that are obsolete;
.... to work with all parts of the federal government to ensure that actions are consistent and coordinated;
.... to make sure the public has a chance to participate in the process of devising new regulations by early notification of proposed regulations and by direct assistance to assure a wide spectrum of participation by consumer and small business groups; and finally;
.... to write regulations in language that people can understand.

The President also set up practical mechanisms to put teeth into these requirements, including the Regulatory Analysis Review Group, the Regulatory Council, and the Interagency Regulatory Liaison Group.

But, unlike Mr. Hardin, all critics are not responsible.

Some are merely using regulatory reform as a kind of shibboleth masking their real motivation, which is to pull the teeth from health and environmental programs. These critics hide their intentions under a flourish of slick public relations sophistries which, for lack of a better word, I might call the immobilization of truth.

Mobil, of course, is the company that has spent hundreds of thousands, if not millions, of dollars over the past few years on a rather strident advertising campaign on the Op-Ed pages of major national newspapers and magazines. Some of the ads give away their true nature by taking the form of fables; others are just as mythical and remote from reality. One such ad attacked government regulators as "new reactionaries," and accused government of trying to "turn back the clock to the detriment of today's standard of living." If I had been writing a headline for that particular ad, my first thought would have been: "Bring Back the Robber Barons."

Since the immobilizers are so misleading, I would like to look for a moment at a few of their favorite debating points.

The first is what I call *Zen analysis*. We all know what is purported to be the way Zen Buddhists sharpen their powers of concentration. First you think of the sound of two hands clapping and then you think of the sound of one hand clapping. It is, I imagine, a very soft sound, somewhat like the quality of reasoning employed by those who subject health, safety, and environmental regulation to a form of one-handed analysis that discovers that, lo and behold, these activities entail a cost.

Of course environmental quality costs money. The immobilizers want us to overlook the fact that the cost of environmental quality is invariably exceeded by the cost of environmental degradation, and that it is the general public who pays the latter, while the former involves some participation by those who would prefer to continue using America the beautiful as a kind of limitless septic field.

For those of us who would rather hear the sound of both hands clapping, I refer you to the *Tenth Annual Report of the Council on Environmental Quality,* and particularly to Chapter 12, which deals with economics.

The data in this chapter, which are objective and which look at every aspect of *both* cost and benefit, including the relevance of dollar yardsticks in assessing quality, conclude:

According to a study done for CEQ the annual benefits realized in 1978 from measured improvements in air quality since 1970 could be reasonably valued at $21.4 billion.

The *Report* also points out that

... The total annual benefits to be enjoyed by 1985 as a result of the nation's water pollution control legislation ... will amount to about $12 billion per year ...

In my estimation, those figures are worth two hands clapping any day.

The second form of sophistry employed by the factual immobilizers involves careful selection of *targets of opportunity.* This involves telling us in great detail about some regulatory excess, and there are some, or about a particular form of regulation that is made to appear unnecessarily burdensome. What never gets mentioned by this form of immobilization is that a great deal of regulation, particularly economic regulation, has come into being because business interests of various kinds *wanted* it or found that it advanced their own goals.

Let me just quote from some remarks by Carol Foreman, Assistant Secretary of Agriculture for Food and Consumer Services. When asked about regulation, she said,

Economic regulation, as practiced by the ICC, and the CAB until recently, and certainly the Securities and Exchange Commission, tends to be heavily supported by industry. Certainly the Packer and Stockyard Administration is heavily supported by industry. Some of that economic regulation tends to raise prices and limit markets, which is exactly what it was intended to do, and the businesses that are regulated love it.

And then she added,

Businessmen generally say health and safety regulations are terrible. They've opposed them. And yet my experience in meat inspection is if somebody were to propose to eliminate meat and poultry inspection, the regulated industries would be the first ones to try to prevent that because we protect them from their competitors who might cheat.

Another favorite way to immobilize the truth involves *scapegoatery*. Thus, when US Steel decides to close 16 plants in eight states, this action is not portrayed as what is bound to happen from time to time in a truly competitive system, or that economic history is largely the pageant of firms that decline and firms that advance, or that disinvestment in the uneconomic is just as important to healthy growth as investment in the economic. Instead, the experience of US Steel is perverted into becoming a horrible example of what happens when government regulation requires environmental protection, or permits foreign competition. What is not stated is that Japanese steel, the major competitor, is produced under environmental protection restrictions that are more stringent than our own, or that trade barriers, high or low, are forms of government regulation.

If the critics really want to reduce the burden of government regulation, they must take steps to eliminate the situations that create the need for regulation. That, it seems to me, is the enlightened response to a changing society. And those companies that are increasingly taking this approach deserve our praise, support and thanks. With this approach, we will be well on our way to an age when, in the words of one editorial writer, we will fit our desires to the environment, and no longer ruin the environment to suit our desires.

CELEBRATION OF SPECIAL TIMES

POPE JOHN PAUL'S MESSAGE[1]

ERIC SEVAREID[2]

The historic week-long visit of Pope John Paul II to the United States on October 1–7 was impressive and inspirational. *Newsweek* declared, "Rarely before had any one visitor or native American commanded American crowds in such vast numbers or moved them so visibly to exhilaration, solemnity, joy, and an outpouring of love" (O. 15, '79, p 3a).

The Pope visited Boston first, then went on to New York, Philadelphia, Des Moines, Chicago, and Washington, D.C. On October 2 and 3, he was greeted by thousands in New York City and watched by millions more on TV. Among other places where he spoke to overflow crowds were the United Nations, Yankee Stadium, St. Patrick's Cathedral, and Shea Stadium.

On October 3 after a rainy ticker tape parade through the city, the Pope paused briefly at the Battery Park to reflect on the significance of the Statue of Liberty, which is visible across the river. He declared that the great monument was "an impressive symbol of what the United States stood for from the very beginning of its history—a symbol of freedom."

Eric Sevareid, the distinguished retired television personality, returned after almost a year to the CBS Evening News program for a special commentary on the Pope's visit. In little more than two minutes, Sevareid conveyed the papal charisma and caught the spirit of the moment. Making a play on Marshall McLuhan's statement that the medium is the message, Sevareid said. "This week the man and his message is the message." As has been his forte through the years, Sevareid expressed the Pope's effects on the crowd eloquently. For another one of Sevareid's commentaries, see *Representative American Speeches*, 1977–1978.

The scene and the man himself seemed of more consequence for this morning's speech than the speech itself. The

---

[1] Delivered on the CBS Evening News, October 3, 1979. © 1979 CBS Inc. All rights reserved. Title supplied by editor.
[2] For biographical note, see Appendix.

Pope of Rome, who used to seem like the Old World incarnate, at New York's Battery where the New World comes to a point.

Here came the great ships in what Thomas Wolfe back in the thirties called the "supreme ecstasy of the modern world, the voyage to America." The ecstasy was the immigrant's feeling of rebirth, the yearning for the second chance. This Pope seems to sense that today America itself yearns for the second chance. That while it has become a successful nation, it is far from a completely successful society or culture.

He knows that the American malaise that President Carter talked about means far more than worries about inflation and energy and leadership. The scriptures said it long ago, "man does not live by bread alone," and in the fullest of material well-being even for the luckiest, there is a sense of life without purpose. That is the nerve end that this happy, believing, positive Pope is touching.

He sees our areas of poverty and human anonymity and our disconnected youth. He was not over flattering in his bow to American generosity, hospitality, and religious freedoms—all that remains. But an American can only wish that the Pope were right in praising what he called our strong family structure and our respect for duty and honest work.

If the central figure were anyone else but this one man, the spectacle we are witnessing would be called by the critics a "media event," non-news news. If the medium itself is often the message, that is because the message is from the traditional sources of government, church, schools have been so faint in recent years and there have been no heroes around.

But this week, the man and his message is the message; the medium is only the medium. John Paul's message is so old that it seems new again. That we were all put on this earth with only one set of instructions to love one another, and that our disobedience has finally made us an endangered species.

Everywhere in the world, people feel this. And everywhere now, people can hear this man's expression of it, because instantaneous mass electronic communication has made the globe a world village.

For this Pope's travels there is no precedent nor for the massive reactions to it. It's as if national leaderships are no longer enough, as if the world is hungering for someone, some idea, some force to take charge of the whole place and give everyone the second chance.

This is Eric Sevareid in Washington.

CAN THE DREAM SURVIVE?[1]

ARCHIBALD COX[2]

The "Fourth-of-July-Oration" is almost as out-of-date as the horse and buggy, but once it attracted "enthusiastic crowds" and elicited "frequent comment in contemporary journals" (see Barnet Baskerville, *The People's Voice*, p 105). The foremost speakers of the day tested their oratorical acumen before their assembled friends and neighbors. In Boston, Massachusetts, this annual event still persists. The celebration includes a parade of the Militia and the reading of the Declaration of Independence from the gallery of the Old State House, as it was in 1776. A formal oration is also a part of the ceremony, and many notable Americans, including John F. Kennedy, have delivered these speeches at Faneuil Hall, a hallowed place, "the cradle of liberty."

On July 4, 1979, Archibald Cox, a distinguished lawyer, Chairman of Common Cause, and a member of the Harvard University Law faculty, was chosen for the honored role. In keeping with the time, the place, and the event, Cox chose as his subject "Can the Dream Survive?" Wise enough to avoid the rhetorical excesses sometimes associated with such speeches, Cox centered his attention upon linking the past and future and making a plea for recommitment to "toleration and cooperation," participation and responsibility. His language was simple; his material was contemporary; his mood was eloquent; and his tone was optimistic.

For an interesting contrast in style, the student of public speaking should compare the Cox speech with one delivered a century ago, perhaps, Edward Everett's "The History of Liberty,"

---

[1] Delivered in Faneuil Hall, Boston, Massachusetts, July 4, 1979. Quoted by permission.
[2] For biographical note, see Appendix.

delivered at Charleston, Massachusetts, in 1827 (*Modern Eloquence*, 1923, X:59–67).

On July 3, 1776, John Adams wrote to Abigail that the day of the signing of the Declaration of Independence "ought to be solemnized with pomp and parade, with shows, games, sports, guns, bells, bonfires and illuminations, from one end of this continent to the other from this time forward forevermore." So it has been, is, and—I trust—will ever be.

None should mistake the meaning of the pomp and parades, or of the sports and illuminations. They are significant only as they express the joyful enthusiasm with which we recommit ourselves to a common vision, a common conviction and a common devotion. As your presence in this hall—the very cradle of liberty—attests, July 4 brings a time when we pause to become conscious of our heritage, when we recall what our forebears—our country—has done for each of us, and when we ask ourselves what we can do for our country—for our children and our children's children—in return.

I

The message carried from Independence Hall in Philadelphia and read from the State House balcony was of the independence of 13 North American colonies from British rule. The vision that set the world afire was of a people's government—in Daniel Webster's words "a government made for the people, made by the people, and answerable to the people." The independence declared was not merely the independence of the North American colonies from British rule. The independence declared was the independence of *all* people from imposed beliefs and imposed rule.

There were those who thought it as foolhardy to stake the future upon the ability of men and women to govern themselves as it was to challenge Great Britain's power. The last republic had perished almost 2000 years before. Yet the Founders' vision was even bolder. They believed and ask us now to believe that man—and woman too—is by nature a rational and social being; that each may grow in nobility and strength through the freedom and responsibility of each to choose the best he can discern; and further, that there is an ideal fitness of things suited to this belief which we have a duty to seek and to do what we can to realize, not just for ourselves but for our children and our children's children. The sense of a continuing adventure—a belief in and commitment to the future, ever-nobler but never-perfect flowering of human spirit—pervaded their words and acts. "I must study politics and war," John Adams wrote, "that my sons may have liberty to study mathematics and philosophy, geography, natural history and naval architecture, navigation, commerce, and agriculture, in order to give their children a right to study painting, poetry, music, architecture, statuary, tapestry, and porcelain."

Such was the faith and the adventure to which the Signers committed first themselves, then their fellows, and ultimately all who pursue the American dream. The Founders and their children, already a diverse lot, were joined and enriched by peoples from many lands. Some came voluntarily in pursuit of the dream—from the green of Ireland, from the Mediterranean shores of Italy, from the mountains of Greece. Others of darker color were cruelly transported as slaves, and only lately allowed to dream.

The adventure prospered—not without conflict and suffering but beyond the fondest expectations. The evidence of its continuing vitality is within the memory of persons in this hall.

Less than 50 years ago the scourge of infantile paralysis still killed tens of thousands of children and doomed more to lives with crippled limbs. The minimum factory wage was not yet 25 cents an hour. There was no social security, no medicare. Men were supposed to be independent and self-reliant, but 20 percent of the work force, one out of five, were unemployed. Hitler's storm troopers were moving toward their zenith with brutality and oppression for all but the master race.

Those evils are remedied. Science and technology cured

some, but it was self-government which moved us closer to realization of the promise of liberty and equality.

First came the New Deal. The practice theory of government were revolutionized. Laissez-faire yielded to social responsibility. Industry and labor were brought under a measure of control. Industrial workers gained new opportunities and new protection. A vast transfer of economic and political power was accomplished. Some of the power has slipped back, I fear, but the transfer was nonetheless tremendous, and much good remains accomplished.

Next with the help of others, came the defeat of Hitler and the reconstruction of Europe.

Then came the civil rights revolution—again within the rule of law. This May 17th we celebrated the 25th anniversary of *Brown vs Board of Education.* After the decision, State laws enforcing a cast system based upon race were invalidated, and their enforcement gradually stopped. New doctrines were developed to extend the reach of the Equal Protection Clause. New federal statutes were enacted curtailing practices restricting equal voting rights, denying equal accommodations, denying equal employment opportunities, and assuring equal housing.

The application of the Equal Protection Clause to the black people revived concern with other inequalities in our national life, especially discrimination against women.

The tasks are unfinished. The resulting bureaucracy seems remote and hard to manage. Revolution carries costs: disappointment as well as hope, frustration as well as benefit, and therefore divisiveness, anger, and even violence. None know the costs better than the people of our city. Yet those who look sharp now see that even in the city which suffered most, moderation returns, and once again we begin to draw together.

Perhaps it is not merely the awareness that comes from having been there [Cox was the director of the Office of the Watergate Special Prosecution Force, 1973] which leads me to add that the Watergate affair provided more evidence of strength in the American system of government than of defects. Given the wrongdoing, our institutions worked. The machinery of justice proved adequate to the vigorous, thorough, but fair investigation and prosecution of charges of pervasive abuse of power in the highest official circles—no mean accomplishment. Even the largely untried, formless mixture of politics and quasi-judicial inquiry called impeachment seemed to work pretty well in the end, so far as there was need to pursue it. The courtroom battles over the Watergate tapes and the firestorm following the Saturday Night Massacre reinforced the constitutional tradition that protects liberty by subjecting all government officials, even the President of the United States, to constitutional restraints and other legal obligations as interpreted by an independent judiciary. Most important of all, Watergate proved the conscience of America. That wrongs were committed in a world characterized by human propensity for evil seems less significant than that the upshot demonstrated that Americans still have the moral sense and idealism associated with their past.

II

Such is our heritage. What of the present?

Self-government could not and cannot succeed without an extraordinary degree of toleration and cooperation. The spirit of liberty is the way of freedom and reason, of mutual trust, civility, and respect for one another. The spirit of liberty is willing to reach conclusions and act upon them until a better hypothesis appears; yet it knows no orthodoxy, it is not too sure that it is right.

To the claim for liberty there was linked—at least in the beginning—a strong sense of individual, personal responsibility. A man should be free, the Founders thought, not because freedom would allow him to pursue his fancy but because freedom permitted him to choose between right and wrong, and thus to exercise man's noblest capacity. A man was responsible for himself and also for the progress of the enterprise. Responsibility went hand in hand not only with liberty but with the opportunity and right of participation.

It was not easy, even in the beginning, to avoid jealousy
and division. Yet toleration and cooperation grew. The hardships of the wilderness taught our forebears that, despite the
value they placed upon individual liberty, they were all fellow voyagers in the same boat, that no person could move
very far towards personal goals unless the vessel moved, and
that the vessel could not move if some voyagers pulled ahead,
some backed water, others demanded a new boat, and more
and more dropped out to go fishing. Ben Franklin put it simply at the signing: "We must all hang together, or assuredly
we shall all hang separately."

Today the external conditions of the adventure in
self-government have changed in ways that obscure the opportunities for participation and responsibility and thus test
our appreciation of essential elements of the Founders' vision.

1. There are more of us. In 1776 there were less than
three million people in the United States. Today there are
200,000,000—a sixty-fold increase. New York City alone has
more than twice the population of the whole United States in
1776. Seattle and Kansas City, each alone, has a population as
large as that of the largest colony, Virginia. The chance of
being heard, or of otherwise exerting a perceptible influence,
has shrunk proportionately. The change diminishes the individual's sense of sharing in a common enterprise to which he
owes an obligation and over which he has a measure of control.

2. Harnessing our natural wealth and the power unlocked
by science and technology required and produced vast aggre-
gations of wealth and human organization which enlarged
and intensified our interdependence. The price of the gains
was to put most of us into the control of others wielding
greater economic power or greater organizational authority.
And the resulting complexity, like our increase in number,
conceals the importance of the individual's contribution.

3. Two hundred years ago Tom Paine could rightly say
that the government which governs least, governs best. If the
peace were kept, the inescapable economic conflicts and adjustments could once be left largely to individual ability, to

the vagaries of nature, and to supposedly impersonal economic forces. In the 1930s, because of the inequality of bargaining power between organizations, on the one hand, and individuals and smaller concerns, on the other hand—between farmers and food processors, between wage-earners and industrial employers, for example—we took the revolutionary decision to temper the conflicts and work out at least portions of the inescapable adjustments through government. Government not only became big and central; it became the forum in which men and women, business corporations and other organized groups contend for individual or group advantage with all the selfishness and ambition, and sometimes the ruthlessness and deceit, which once characterized the marketplace.

These three great changes are unalterable facts.

We cannot cut a population of 200,000,000 back to 3,000,-000.

We yearn for simplicity and there is hope for a return to simpler values, but nostalgia should not blind us to the enormous gains in the fight against ignorance, poverty, and disease which flow from complex technologies and industrtial organization.

Nor is it likely that we shall strip big government of the power to mediate between clashing social and economic interests and return the process of adjustment to the marketplace. Too much is gained, when economic power is unequal, by putting the contest in a forum relatively open to public scrutiny, where men who are somewhat more disinterested and are charged with a sense of justice and the general welfare can exercise some influence, and where every now and then someone or something can lift the public spirit to meet a great occasion.

III

Given the changes, what have those who met here and in Independence Hall to say to us.

They were realists. They would tell us first to face the

facts—to realize that even though the opportunities for responsible participation are obscured by size and complexity, in truth interdependence grows and with it the need for participation, toleration, and cooperation.

The current fashion is to turn away from government. The Founders would admonish us—I think—to give more heed to how government works. As students of history and experienced and intensely practical politicians, they had unique appreciation of the long-range importance of governmental institutions and procedures. They would find it strange that our extraordinary progress in unlocking the physical secrets of the universe has had no parallel in discoveries of better ways to govern ourselves. In our time, while we have vastly increased the powers of government and the bounty it can dispense, we have neglected to search for the institutional measures that could at least help to preserve, and now to revive the individual's meaningful participation in the common enterprise. At the very least, in a time when calls for "sunset laws" and examination of every governmental measure for its inflationary impact are the fashion, we could put every measure to a further test: Is the measure framed in the way which provides the widest opportunities for meaningful participation by localities and citizens and which gives the greatest encouragement to their sense of responsibility and power of decision.

The Founders would add—I am confident—that by extending the public financing of election campaigns from the Presidential candidates to contests for Senator and Representative in Congress we could take our government away from the special interests that presently finance the extravagant cost of packaging and selling professional political candidates and to give it back to the people.

Do not the Founding Fathers also tell us to demand more of our elected officials? Not more laws. Not more remedies. Quick solutions, packaged to the hour or half-hour in advance, are found only on the television screen. The men we elect are neither better nor worse than us; they reflect ourselves and our limitations. But surely we could demand more openness, more candor in stating facts, more consistency in speaking to different groups, more forthrightness in helping us to understand the choices we must make and the limits on our power. Thomas Jefferson wrote that men are divided into two parties: (1) those who fear and distrust the people and wish to draw all powers from them; (2) those who identify themselves with the people, have confidence in them, cherish and consider them as the most honest and safe. Those of the first party perhaps would join with President Nixon whose lawyers wrote in one of the briefs filed in support of the claim of executive privilege that—

The right of Presidential confidentialilty is not a mystical prerogative. It is, rather, the raw essence of the Presidential process, the institutionalized recognition of the crucial role played by human personality in the negotiation, *manipulation* and disposition of human affairs.

The word "manipulation" revealed the evil.

Those Presidents and officials of the second philosophy see their responsibility as providing the people with the information and analysis necessary to make their own decisions. However the fuel shortage may have been manipulated for private gain, its core is neither myth nor conspiracy. Dependence upon foreign sources for energy to fuel homes, industries, and automobiles *will* force radical changes in the American economy and our personal lives. Our ability to adjust, our willingness to contribute to common good, depends upon a much blunter, more specific, more forthright exposition of our situation and concrete choices than any yet supplied. Only then can we make the people's self-governing decisions.

Most important of all—I believe—those who look down upon today's celebrants of independence would admonish us to remember Benjamin Franklin's advice that most assuredly we shall all hang separately unless we all hang together. When the spirit of toleration and cooperation declines, factions press to achieve their separate aims not through general progress but taking from each other, and they end by defeating themselves as well as others. We shall not solve the energy crisis by each seeking to outdo the other in securing gasoline and diesel fuel. The independent truckers' strike reminds us of the drastic readjustments we face and the need to mitigate hardships, but it also warns of the danger in tearing the fabric of social cooperation. The injustices of inflation have taught millions that the harder they work the farther they fall behind, but we shall not learn to deal with this curse of bigness either, if each group races to secure a greater wage or a higher price than any other.

IV

Toleration and cooperation require more than the sense of personal participation and responsibility which I have tried to suggest. They depend in the end upon belief in the value of the common enterprise and upon trust in its conduct and in others who participate.

I grant you that confidence in the value and future success of the enterprise comes harder today than formerly. The quick conquest of a continent, the industrial and technological revolutions, and our might in two wars bred a folklore of endless resources and easy success. For all but the unfortunate, technology and industrial organization poured out a seemingly endless flow of material comforts. American might in two wars led us to suppose that our power extended to the farthest reaches of the globe. Recent decades dispelled these illusions. Our cities deteriorate. Our power in the world is limited. Foreign powers control the natural resources at the base of our economy and personal habits.

Ironically, our very success intensifies the drain upon our spirit. In the beginning misfortune and suffering were inexorable as sewing and reaping, or birth and death. Should the plague come, should the crops fail, still one trusting in ultimate mercy could say with the Psalmist, "The judgments of the Lord are true and righteous altogether." Now the sense of inevitability is gone. Man feels that man is in charge, he is in charge as never in all history—man with his limitations, his faults and perversity.

We have lost our innocence and learned our capacity for evil. Witness the corruption and self-seeking in government, the bombs dropped on Southeast Asia, and the gap that still exists between our pretenses and practices in the treatment of blacks, chicanos, and native Americans.

It takes honesty and courage to face these facts. It is to our credit that we have the honesty and courage to look in the mirror and see ourselves as we are.

Our mistake is to suppose that we are the first to face these perceptions. Our danger is that we become obsessed by human failings, lose perspective, and forget the true nature of the enterprise bequeathed to us. Contemporary literature and the arts tell of man the absurd, the pervert, and the drop-out, but rarely of man the hero or even the tragic, for the tragic requires a degree of nobility and it is the fashion to forget Prometheus' reach and see only the chains.

But we are not the first. "We are not to be translated . . . to liberty in a featherbed." So Jefferson responded to the bleak reality of 1790. The Founders had no illusions about human weaknesses, especially the temptations corrupting those with great power over other men. They did not use Pogo's words, "We have met the enemy and he is us," but their religion taught them the same truth in the language of original sin. The men and women who later sought freedom across the seas, who crossed the prairies and the great plains to conquer the mountains and build gardens in the desert, also knew the costs, the struggle, the defeats, and disappointments. They too knew their own fallibility and capacity for evil. But enough had the still greater insight to keep alive the vision of a constant flowering of humane society, and they also had the still greater courage to pursue their vision even when they knew that neither they nor their children, nor their children's children, could ever wholly achieve it.

Our mountains are the size and complexity of the organizations which we must manage to enjoy the wealth unlocked by the industrial, scientific, and technological revolutions. Our desert wastelands are the belief in the quick fix, the affluence that blinds us to our mutual dependence, the rapidity of the social and moral change which cuts us off from where we have been yet does not tell us where we go. Still, the voice which spoke to our predecessors calls to us:

> Something hidden. Go and find it.
> Go and look behind the ranges.
>
> Something lost behind the ranges,
> Lost and waiting for you. Go!

OPTIMISM ABOUT THE FUTURE[1]

Clare Boothe Luce[2]

On October 10, 1979, Clare Boothe Luce became the first woman to receive the Sylvanus Thayer Award of the United States Military Academy in recognition of her service to her country. Others so honored in the past have included John Foster Dulles (1959), Henry Cabot Lodge (1960), Dwight D. Eisenhower (1961), Douglas MacArthur (1962), Francis Cardinal Spellman (1967), Bob Hope (1968), Billy Graham (1972), and James R. Killian, Jr. (1978). It was an appropriate time for Mrs. Luce to receive the award and, as she was careful to point out to the "Gentlemen of the Corps," that "There are women in all four classes at this time."

The ceremonies of the day were dramatic. Following an afternoon parade of the Corps of Cadets, Mrs. Luce was presented with an engraved sabre. Later at dinner in Washington Hall, before the assembled cadets and staff, she became the twenty-second recipient of the Thayer Award (a gold medal and a scroll), and she responded.

The speech, autobiographical in the opening paragraphs, makes excellent use of contrast to establish "the speed with which America achieved, political, economic, and military superiority in the first half of this century." After ennumerating the problems that the nation faces today she becomes optimistic in her closing

---

[1] Delivered on the evening of October 10, 1979, at a banquet in Washington Hall, US Military Academy, West Point, New York. Quoted by permission. Title supplied by editor. From *Congressional Record*, October 31, 1979, p S15581-82.
[2] For biographical note, see Appendix.

paragraph. She is confident that democracy will be saved by what Jefferson called "the natural aristocracies of brains and talent," and that there will be "a rebirth of that national will and sense of high purpose that has carried America safely through all the other crises of our history." She had touched upon a conservative theme that is appreciated by the military establishment.

General Goodpaster, General Finlay, Ladies and Gentlemen of the Corps, Distinguished Guests:

Everyone desires and needs the good opinions of others to be happy. I have sometimes lived for days on a sincere compliment. But nothing so nourishes our spirits as recognition by those we hold in highest esteem. I will thrive on this honor you have done me the rest of my days.

But although it goes straight to my heart, I'm trying not to let it go to my head. I know I do not rate with the heroic figures who have been given the Sylvanus Thayer Award. I am a brave woman. But I am no heroine. I am nevertheless profoundly grateful to you for bestowing Fame on me by association.

I suspect that the fact that this is the first year that there are women in all four classes is not unrelated to my good fortune. No doubt the Graduates' Association wanted the women of the Corps who stay the course to know they will be welcomed, and no honors barred, to the officer class of the world's finest military professionals. And what better way to flag this message than to give the Thayer Award to a woman? I am just damned lucky I was chosen to be that first woman.

I know that the women of the Corps will see to it that I'm not the last, and that, in course of time, they will produce from their own ranks, a first-rate heroine.

Now at this point, custom requires the recipient of the Award to make a few remarks born of personal experience.

Well, I don't want for experience of living. I have lived more than a third of all the years since the signing of the Declaration of Independence. It was the last third, in case you are wondering; and it has included all but three years of this century—the first three.

The principal thing I've learned in my lifetime is that you and I, and all Americans are living in the best of all centuries, the best of all countries, and under the best of all forms of government.

The material progress that the United States has made in just the last 50 years is the marvel of all ages, and the envy of all peoples.

I was born in New York City in the prime years of the gas-light, wood-bin, coal scuttle, pump handles, outhouse, horse-and-buggy era. My grandparents and parents believed like everyone else in my childhood that America was destined to become—in say a century or so, a country as great as any of the mighty powers of Europe.

My grandfather, who owned the largest livery stable in Hoboken, was absolutely certain that in another decade there would be two horses and carriages in every man's stable.

But certain tho' my grandfather was of progress, he would have sent for the horsedrawn booby-wagon if someone had tried to convince him that in just a few decades, people in London or Tokyo could sit in their living-rooms and see and hear the President making a speech from the White House; that men would be walking on the moon; that millions and millions of Americans would be tripping around the globe in flying machines; that surgeons would be able to swap old hearts for new and reattach severed limbs; that the vast Colonial Empires of all the great powers would be lying in ruins, and that America, following her victories in two world wars, would emerge at mid-20th century the greatest, richest, strongest power the world had ever known.

The speed with which America achieved political, economic, and military superiority in the first half of this century would have made my grandfather a little dizzy—had he lived to see it. But he would have had no trouble explaining why it happened. He and my grandmother had come to America in the 1800s (as had about 40 million other immigrants) to find Liberty. He knew that Liberty has no meaning save as it means Freedom for the individual—religious freedom, political freedom, economic freedom; and he knew the proper goal of these freedoms is to give the individual the chance to become what he or she is capable of becoming.

My grandfather would have had no trouble understanding that the miracle of progress America made in the first half of this century was produced by a free political and economic system which had released the physical and mental energies of millions of people.

Well, some of you are thinking, if this is such a glorious century, and America is such a great country, and we have such a fine form of government, how come we are in so much trouble today?

Well, Theodore Roosevelt—my first President, told Americans more than 30 years ago how the country might get into the kind of trouble we are in.

"The things that will destroy America," he warned, "are prosperity-at-any-price, safety-first instead of duty-first, the love of soft living, and the get-rich-quick theory of life." And, "if we seek merely swollen, slothful ease" and accept "ignoble peace," then he said, "bolder and stronger people will pass us by, and will win for themselves the domination of the world."

Our democratic form of government is the highest form known to man. But it requires the highest type of human nature—a type which has always and everywhere been in the minority. Yet it is always the majority that chooses, not only the course, but the leaders who are then pledged to follow it. The majority has—at least in the last decade increasingly chosen "prosperity-at-any-price and safety-first instead of duty-first." The majority have ceased to be patriots, for patriotism, as Theodore Roosevelt saw it, is the sense of collective responsibility for the economic stability and the military security of the nation.

We seem to have entered that period which history tells us always marks the hour of greatest danger to a democracy. This is when its citizens persist in raiding their own treasury, and when faced with a strong and avowed enemy—"a bolder and stronger people"—they substitute the ideal of peace for the idea of national security.

It is then that a democracy is doomed to depression and defeat unless it is rescued from its follies of its unthinking majority by those thinking minorities which Thomas Jefferson called "The natural aristocracies of brains and talent."

West Point exists to train and educate an aristocracy of military leaders. You are today the best military educational institution in the country.

So you know that the condition of our military establishment in relation to that of the USSR is real cause for alarm; that American power, both nuclear and conventional, has been steadily eroding since the mid-60; and that if this trend is not soon—and sharply—reversed, the US will probably become a second, perhaps even a third-rate power before this century is ended.

Your study of military history has also taught you that an ally is a friend you can always count on to count on you. If our NATO allies should become convinced that our military power—in relation to the USSR's—is irreversibly crumbling, they will—indeed, they must as a matter of survival—design their own policies of Detente and collaboration with the Kremlin, and you may be sure, these will leave us isolated in our own hemisphere, and tragically vulnerable to attack.

But it is certainly arguable that the conquest of the US by force of arms is not likely in this century. For even if our military position grows considerably weaker, we would still retain a fearsome nuclear second-punch capacity.

What now seems more likely to happen is the collapse of our industrial system, which is today not only inflation ridden, but is over 50 percent dependent on Middle East oil. The truly shameful and humiliating fact is that six years after the Arab oil embargo, our government still has no realistic policy—political or military—for securing our access to Arab oil in the amounts, no less at the prices, necessary to maintain the productivity of our economy.

Congress and the media together have virtually destroyed the capacity of our Intelligence Services to intervene covertly in foreign countries in the effort to prevent anti-American forces from bringing down friendly governments. So if tomorrow Saudi and Kuwait should go the way of Iran, we could do nothing to prevent it—short of war—and we would be plunged into a depression far worse than that of the '30s, from which there could be no issuance save war, or political submission—and dependence on the Soviet Union—the only oil self-sufficient industrial nation in the world today.

Can we turn things around before it is too late to spare our country suffering, humiliation, or war?

I am an optimist, although in my experience the principal difference between optimists and pessimists is that pessimists are generally better informed. But optimism about the future is reasonable. For the future is always uncertain, and good things as well as bad can happen. Indeed, only one good thing need happen to turn things around: a rebirth of that national will and sense of high purpose that has carried America safely through all the other great crises in our history.

"Every true man," wrote Emerson, "is a cause, a country and an age."

No rebirth of will or purpose, or patriotism are needed here at West Point.

Members of the Corps, you are of that true and happy breed who have a cause in life who have accepted freely the stern disciplines of mind and body that will make you successful in that mission, and who have the courage, if your country should require it, to risk your lives in its cause. You know why you are living, what you are doing, and who you are doing it for. The path of honor, duty, country, is a hard one, but a straight one. You'll find no one on it going around in circles lost and confused, as so many people these days are. And you will enjoy all your lives the respect and the gratitude of your countrymen.

I thank you, with all my heart, for that parade on the plain. This has been the proudest and happiest day of my life.

My only regret is that I will not live long enough to see much of you on that long gray line become the great soldier-statesmen, soldier-scholars, or soldier's soldiers of tomorrow. Would you please remember me maybe once when you do?

IN CELEBRATION OF THE INAUGURATION OF THE SUSAN B. ANTHONY COIN[1]

Elizabeth Holtzman[2]

On July 2, 1979, Representative Elizabeth Holtzman was the keynote speaker at the Susan B. Anthony luncheon. The event, attended by 800 at the Rochester Chamber of Commerce commemorated the introduction of the Susan. B. Anthony one-dollar coin, honoring the great suffragette (1820–1906). Representative Holtzman observed, "This coin was the first United States coin to bear the likeness of a real woman, a long-time resident of Rochester and a great New Yorker."

Miss Holtzman, a four-term Congresswoman from New York's Sixteenth District, spoke with "feeling" about the event and received "a strong and lengthy applause" (Machacek, Rochester, NY *Times Union*, Jl. 3, '79). A leader in the equal rights movement as well as other liberal causes, she is a founder and co-chairwoman of the Congress Woman's Caucus, a bi-partisan group which is dedicated to improving the social and legal status of women. Among her colleagues she is known as "a hardworking legislator," (*Almanac of American Politics, 1980*, p 604) certainly the opposite from the stereotyped New York City politician. In appearance, she is described as "unostentatiously attractive . . . five feet, three inches tall" with "shoulder-length auburn hair," giving "the impression of some reserved heroine from another-century English novel" (*Christian Science Monitor*, Jl. 26 '74).

The speech, a fitting model of a speech of commemoration, is well-organized into four distinct parts: first, a brief recognition of the immediate occasion; second, ample historical background for what Miss Anthony did and stood for; third, a discussion of what today's women's rights advocates must do; and fourth, a brief, but persuasive appeal to carry on the "struggle for human rights, for human dignity and human liberty."

Representative Holtzman's views are expanded in an earlier speech entitled "Women and Equality Under the Law," found in *Representative American Speeches, 1976–1977*.

---

[1] Keynote address at the Susan B. Anthony luncheon, of the Area Chamber of Commerce, Rochester, New York, at noon, July 2, 1979. Quoted by permission.

[2] For biographical notes, see Appendix.

It is a great pleasure to be here. Indeed, there is no place else I would rather be today than in Rochester joining with you in this wonderful celebration.

We Americans have always been accused of worshipping the Almighty Dollar, and today, together, we can unashamedly and unabashedly plead guilty.

Because now we finally have a dollar that is really worth something.

But I must warn you. You can't tell this special value from the heft of the coin—actually, it's a good bit smaller than other dollar coins—"daintier" some might say. And its chink in your pocket may not be as loud or robust—"masculine" if you will—as quarters or half dollars. You won't even find a familiar buffalo or president's face on it. And surely it will buy less in the marketplace than any dollar we've had in the past 20 years.

So what is there to celebrate? Lots!

This is the first United States coin to bear the likeness of a real woman—Susan B. Anthony, a long-time resident of Rochester and a great New Yorker. In honoring this extraordinary American, the coin honors the best in all of us and the best our country stands for.

Susan almost didn't make it onto the face of the coin because Miss Liberty was the Treasury Department's first choice. But we prevailed. Our new dollar coin depicts not an allegorical figure but a real woman who devoted her life to the struggle for liberty.

Perhaps Susan was picked because she really understood the value of a dollar—to women, that is. At a time when women were viewed as the property of their husbands, she launched a state-wide campaign that forced New York State to allow married women to control the dollars they earned.

Susan B. Anthony hated tyranny. She fought her first fight against the tyranny of alcohol. And she learned her first lesson in feminism when the Temperance movement barred women from speaking at meetings or holding office in the organization. She championed the abolition of slavery, and denounced the physical tyranny of human beings over each other. But when the Civil War was won, she discovered that those who wanted to free the slaves sneered at the thought of rights for women.

But she was not daunted or embittered or stymied. Susan B. Anthony learned about liberty from those who preached it for men only, and with an infallible intelligence and relentless logic, she applied those lessons to her cause.

Susan B. Anthony hated hypocrisy. She confronted America with the words and spirit of its Constitution, challenging the nation to live up to these magnificent principles. In 1872, inspired by an editorial in the Rochester *Democrat* and *Chronicle* which exhorted everyone to vote (the right to vote had just been guaranteed to former slaves), Susan B. Anthony decided that she too could exercise the franchise. Leading a contingent of Rochester women, she registered and voted. Shortly afterwards, she was arrested by a male US Marshal and tried by a male prosecutor before a male judge and an all male jury.

At her trial, Susan B. Anthony argued that women were covered by the 14th Amendment, providing due process and equal protection of the law to all persons, and the 15th Amendment, giving voting rights to citizens. Her words are worth remembering:

"I hoped for a broad and liberal interpretation of the Constitution and its recent amendments which should declare all US citizens under its protecting aegis—which should declare equality of rights the national guarantee to all persons born or naturalized in the United States."

Susan B. Anthony lost. The term "person" in the 14th Amendment, and "citizen" in the 15th Amendment did not, the court ruled, include women. She was convicted and fined—like Henry David Thoreau, she was forced to become a lawbreaker because she sought to make America put into practice for all people the ideals of liberty and justice on which it was founded.

She continued for the rest of her life to play a monumental role in the struggle for women's suffrage, but she died without the joy of seeing women enfranchised.

So we honor Susan B. Anthony for her courage, her indomitable spirit, her tenacious work for women, and her confidence that America would, in the end, do what was right.

She was reviled, ridiculed, and despised during her lifetime. But she was never deterred.

We honor her struggle and we honor the cause she labored for so valiantly.

But the true value of the Susan B. Anthony dollar lies not in just reminding us of the work she did but of what we must do. The work she started—to base relations between men and women on mutual respect and not on domination and aggression—is unfinished.

Indeed, if Susan B. Anthony returned today, I think she would be both pleased and chagrined, glad of some progress, saddened by how much still needs doing.

Yes, women finally won the right to vote. But the term "persons" in the 14th Amendment still does not fully apply to women. As the Supreme Court said recently in the *Bakke* case, the 14th Amendment does not protect women from sex discrimination as it protects blacks from race discrimination. And so, the Supreme Court allows young girls to be excluded from technical high schools and women to be excluded from pregnancy coverage in insurance policies.

Susan B. Anthony would insist that women must be placed firmly in the Constitution. She would argue that the Equal Rights Amendment must be ratified. And it must be. As we stand here today, let us pledge our first Susan B. Anthony dollars to ensure ratification of the ERA. We can and should be proud that New York State has ratified the ERA, but we must not be complacent. We must pitch in and help in the effort to get three more states to ratify. We cannot permit our own rights and the rights of future generations to be jeopardized by a handful of people in three state legislatures.

Susan B. Anthony would be surprised to find that women still suffer inequities in the workplace. Although women now make up 41 percent of the work force, we earn, generally, less than 60 percent of what men earn. The Equal Pay Act and

Title VII of the Civil Rights Act are riddled with loopholes and cannot assure equality in employment.

Marital property rights are still a concern. Just recently, the New York State legislature refused to recognize that a husband and wife contribute equally to the marriage as an economic entity. As a consequence, proposed legislation could give a pittance in divorce property settlements to wives who are homemakers or who earn less than their husbands. [New New York law (July '79) decrees "equitable" distribution of property.]

Discrimination persists in insurance, in credit opportunities, pension rights, and Social Security. Rape laws remain archaic and frequently leave women with little hope of legal recourse. Society has only just begun to understand the phenomenon of battered wives, and programs to protect these women are inadequate. We need better efforts to help displaced homemakers.

If Susan were brought to trial now, she would find much that was sadly familiar. Not only would she have no assurance that the 14th Amendment would apply to her, but the judge, the prosecutor and the US Marshal would probably still be men (only 4 percent of federal judges are women, and fewer than that are prosecutors or marshals).

Many of us who carry on her work today are also ridiculed and scorned. "Women's lib" has become a "put-down," a sneering way of summing up and dismissing the women's rights movement. Nevertheless we, like Susan B. Anthony, remain undeterred. After all, it was those who arrested and convicted her who suffer history's guilty verdict. Those who today arrest and stymie the effort for full rights for women will suffer the same fate 100 years from now.

So, as we stand here, 73 years after Susan Anthony's death, we recognize that we have much to do.

The question for us is: will the struggle be confined to a small, courageous but lonely band of women? Will the rest of America sit on the sidelines? Or will the goal of full equality for women be one that engages all of us.

This is for you to answer. The coin has value only if everyone accepts it.

Let us remember that this struggle, after all, is not for women only. It is a struggle for human rights, for human dignity and human liberty.

It is a struggle that cannot and will not be lost. As Susan B. Anthony said, "Failure is impossible." And those who sit on the sidelines do so at their peril. [*Editor's note:* The coin did not meet with public approval so coinage has been suspended temporarily.]

CONSCIENCE AND COMMITMENT

SERVICE TO OTHERS[1]

THEODORE M. HESBURGH[2]

Father Theodore M. Hesburgh, the President of the University of Notre Dame and perhaps the best academic speaker today, has spoken on many college campuses as attested to by his seventy honorary degrees.

This speech was delivered at the 110th Commencement held in Special Events Center, at the University of Utah, Salt Lake City, at 9:30 A.M. on June 9, 1979. His audience of over 10,000 consisted of graduates from sixteen colleges with their parents and friends. "Unfailingly optimistic" (*Time Magazine*, My. 2, '77) and forward looking, he called upon the graduates to commit themselves to "voluntary non-profit good works" or service to others, in order to benefit the less fortunate and to enrich life and community.

His address is a good model from the point of view of its conception and composition. The line of thought is introduced in typical commencement style that is particularly appropriate, in light of the troubled confusion of many in these times. The organization is clearly discernable and advances his thought, each part leading directly to the next. His well-chosen examples, in vivid and impressive language, amplify his points and add interest to what he is saying. The speech, probably under twenty minutes, is well-suited to a commencement program and offers serious recommendations without becoming "preachy."

This is a day and an occasion on which all of you graduates tend to think long thoughts: a chapter of your life ending, a new one beginning; something accomplished, something yet to be done; a time for planning, dreaming, hoping. It is also for some of you a time of uncertainty, nostalgia, even fear. I suppose that each one of you graduates has thought in your

[1] Delivered at 110th Commencement, University of Utah, Salt Lake City at 9:30 A.M., June 9, 1979 in the Special Events Center. Quoted by permission.
[2] For biographical note, see Appendix.

more quiet moments, what is to become of me and what will be the value of my life?

I cannot help you much with the first question, because I am not a prophet and I do not know—only God does—what will become of you in the years ahead. I can say something about the second question, what will be the value of your life, wherever you go, whatever you do.

Before doing so, let me try to put all of your lives in perspective. First, you have an abundance of reasons to be grateful. You might have been born in Neanderthal times when human life was brief and brutal. You might have been born in the dark ages when there was little culture and less hope. For most of mankind's history, and for most of the men and women who have ever lived on earth, life has meant a daily sun rise to sun set effort just to sustain physical existence, not to enrich it, or much less enjoy it. They have survived for awhile, have not lived humanly at all.

For some reason you and I cannot explain, we were born in the most advanced and civilized age that mankind has yet known. Moreover, we find ourselves living in the most developed and affluent nation on earth.

So far, so good, but the blessings of all this prosperity are not unmixed. We in America have our special temptations. We enjoy an enormous freedom to do something with our lives, but we are, because of our times, pulled in many different directions: to seek security even though it may mean a bland existence; to seek physical pleasure at all costs even though this means a superficial and selfish life; to seek money and material gain alone, even though we have been taught that spiritual achievement is of a much higher and more fulfilling order. We may also seek power for its own sake, a heady adventure, but chancy unless we have a fairly clear idea and intention about the use of power. None of these goals: security, pleasure, wealth, or power are bad or evil in themselves. They vitiate our lives only if they become ends in themselves, without higher goals that lift them to a nobler purpose. Seek any of them for themselves alone, and they will empty your life of value, whatever power you wield, what-

ever wealth or pleasure you enjoy. History books are full of
leaders who have wielded power for its own sake and left
millions of ruined lives in their wake. Hitler is a classic example in our century.

The greatest freedom you enjoy today is to choose your
own goals for your own lives, goals that will enrich both you
and your times whatever wealth, power, or pleasure you will
enjoy in the years to come. I would like to suggest one goal
that has served our country, our world, and our fellow
humans well. For want of a better term, I will just call it
"service to others."

Years ago, de Tocqueville found this virtue of service to
others one of the most redeeming features of American life.
He remarked that when Americans discovered a problem,
they just got together and did something about it. In the years
since he wrote, volunteerism has given us all of the great religious and secular endeavors that enrich the life of this country, hospitals and universities, myriads of professional societies for lawyers, doctors, teachers, youth activities of every
kind, scouts, 4-H, Y.M.C.A., C.Y.O., clubs, service organizations, associations for good works on every level of local and
national life.

In the great grey world of socialism, everything is done by
the state, nothing is private or voluntary. Here we do the
most important things for ourselves. In fact, if all private volunteer activities were to cease today, it would affect all our
lives far more than if the federal government—the greatest
public power—suddenly ceased to exist. In fact, it would be
interesting to contrast the good done by the billions given to
voluntary non-profit good works with the results of the much
greater amount given through federal taxation.

Who can measure the good will and generosity that inspire and sustain all these beneficial voluntary activities? All
we can say for sure is that unless millions of Americans
pitched in and made them work, there would be none of
them, no churches, no political parties, no agriculture, no Red
Cross or United Fund, no newspapers, radio, or television, no
operas, ballet, or orchestras, no museums or galleries, not
even any zoos.

Volunteerism, the great American virtue of giving something of one's self to help others, has certainly served America well. It has been suggested that your generation will not sustain all these good works, since this is called the "me" generation, with its own best seller, "Looking Out for Number One."

I don't believe that. Better than a third of our student body at Notre Dame spends untold hours each week in myriad tasks of voluntarism helping the young and old, the retarded, the sick, and the unfortunate. If I had my way, service to others less fortunate would be an expected and integral part of education for all Americans, not just in service to Americans, but to the world as well. I think it is part of the dues we should pay for our great good fortune as a nation. It may even be, for all the new generations to come, the only real way of keeping America great and of redeeming our times.

Allow me to suggest to you three qualities, intimately associated with the volunteer spirit, that I would hope you might make part of your lives in the days to come, to assure your lives and yourselves of value and quality.

First, compassion. This really means the human quality of sensitivity, to suffer with those who suffer, to be moved, to reach out, to understand, to want to help, to serve. We find the opposite of compassion in the story of the Good Samaritan.

The priest and the levite, both supposedly religious persons, saw the poor fellow who had been set upon by robbers on the road to Jericho, beaten and left helpless. The priest and the levite looked and passed on. They didn't want to get involved—like so many moderns who pass by accidents on the highway or look the other way when someone is in trouble in our big cities. The Good Samaritan, however, looked and was moved by compassion. He bound up the poor fellow's wounds, brought him to the nearest inn, and paid for his care. Jesus told that story when He was asked, "Who is my neighbor?"

In a shrinking and highly interdependent world, everyone is our neighbor: especially the billion unfortunates of the

Fourth World who are hungry every day, who are illiterate, who never see a doctor from birth to death, who live in cardboard shacks or mud and wattle huts, who have to live each year on less money than most of us will spend this weekend. Like ourselves, all of these billion unfortunates are human, as are our own American unfortunates who live in our affluent country's too numerous pockets of poverty. Unlike us, all of these, like the man beaten and robbed on the road to Jericho, have little hope, unless we look upon them and are moved to compassion.

However, compassion alone will not do it, unless joined to another quality that I recommend to you for all of your lives today, namely, commitment. We are told by the so-called wise ones of our generation that it is neither cool nor clever to commit oneself to anything. Maybe that explains why we have almost as many divorces as marriages in America today. It takes real commitment to love enough to say and to mean: "for better or for worse, for richer or for poorer, in sickness or in health, until death do us part." Commitment is very much akin to love and the measure of love is to love without measure, especially in giving ourselves to others less fortunate. Calculation never made a hero.

Albert Schweitzer, a true hero of our times, was a promising theologian, a concert organist, a medical doctor as well. He loved those less fortunate and most needy enough to leave Europe and his triple career there to serve those without any medical care at Lambarene in what was then French Equatorial Africa. I do not know what fame he might have achieved in Europe, but he inspired all the world for what he did in that remote village on the shore of a turgid African river.

One of our students, Tom Dooley, was inspired by Schweitzer to give up a promising career here at home to give his life and medical skill to literally hundreds of thousands of unfortunates who otherwise would have been without medical care in Southeast Asia. I was with Tom on his thirty-fourth birthday, in Sloan-Kettering Memorial Cancer Hospital in New York. He died the next day, leaving a dozen hospitals he established in the poorer parts of this planet. Not a long life, but it had a quality all its own.

We cannot all make the commitments of a Schweitzer or a Dooley. But without some measure of compassion and commitment, we are likely to live for ourselves alone and that is a poor and valueless life indeed.

The third and last quality I would recommend to you today is consecration. This is obviously and admittedly a religious word and reality. I make no apology for it because I personally find the other two qualities of compassion and commitment very difficult to achieve in life, unless buttressed by religious motivation. Transcending, unaided by divine grace, the overwhelming urge to personal selfishness and self-centeredness is something I cannot honestly advise you to try. I think the Lord was telling us this when He said we have to lose our lives to find them. We lose them in service to others and find ourselves much enriched by what we have given away.

Once more, a story is worth a thousand words. One of our students was spending his summer on the altiplano of Peru working on a social project there. One morning, as he walked along the shore of Lake Titicaca to the clinic where he worked, he passed an Indian hut and a little girl of four or five ran down the path to see him. He knelt down to talk to her, face to face, and found that she did not even speak Spanish, only Quichua, the Indian language of the high Peruvian plateau. As he looked at her, his faith was deeply shaken. It is cold at 14,000 feet. He had a warm jacket on, she, only a thin cotton dress. He had eaten a decent breakfast, she would be lucky to get a crust of bread all day. He was a university student, she would be not only illiterate in the language of her country, but in her own as well. He had high hopes for the future, she could only face a short, hard, painful, and hopeless life.

How can there be a God, he thought, with such injustice, such inequity, in this world? Then he remembered the stirring words of the Gospel, the ultimate judgment on each of our lives. "I was hungry and you gave Me to eat, I was thirsty and you gave Me to drink, I was naked and you clothed Me, I was in prison and you visited Me, I was a stranger and you took Me in. Whensoever you did this to one of these, the least of My brethren, you did it to Me."

That young man completed his education, fulfilled the compassion and commitment of that moment by the lake side, and is consecrating his professional efforts today in a distant and very poor land for the betterment of his neighbors there. I like to think he is loving and serving God, too, by all he does for others. And I know that while all he does is of great temporal value, fulfilling him today, it is also, and more importantly, of eternal value as well. Consecration says all that.

You do not have to go afar to serve others. All around are those in need. They need teachers as well as doctors, lawyers as well as social workers, mostly they need compassionate, committed, consecrated neighbors and friends. Wherever you go, whatever you do, you will always find people in need of something you can give, if you will.

Is all of this too idealistic to be true? Let me say to each of you, in conclusion, the truest advice I know. One day, on a trip back to Europe, Dr. Albert Schweitzer was asked to address a graduating class like yours today. His words were few, for his life was his message. He simply said: "I do not know where all of you are going or what you will do, but let me tell you simply this: unless you set aside some portion of your lives to help and serve those less fortunate than yourselves, you will really not be happy."

My best wish and prayer for all of you today is simply this: May you all find, in all your various ways, the wonderful secret of happy lives in serving others.

"BE A FLAKE ... ON BEHALF OF SOMEBODY OR SOMETHING"[1]

LOWELL P. WEICKER JR.[2]

On June 15, 1979 at 3 P.M., Senator Lowell P. Weicker Jr. (Republican, Conn.) took part in the commencement exercises in the gym of the Brunswick School, a boy's private day school in Greenwich, Connecticut. He addressed an audience of 400, made up of the graduates, including his oldest son, friends and family. Any speaker who has had the experience of trying to please, but not embarrass, a member of his own family at such a time, will confirm how difficult such an assignment is.

The speech, less than twenty minutes (appropriate for such an occasion), seems informal and almost casual in substance, language, and mood, but the construction and content deserve careful study. On examination, it is well conceived and designed to sustain interest. In order to establish rapport with his youthful listeners (about 150 juniors and seniors), who are often not too tolerant of commencement addresses, he chose to make his point in familiar, colloquial language out of their vocabularies. His eight examples, of living up to your lone convictions were well-known to his listeners, who tended to support his proposition:

"Be a flake, a loner, a kook, a maverick on behalf of somebody or something."

I volunteered for this duty last fall and now that the moment has arrived to speak before son, family, mother, friends—in the home town—the barracks wisdom of my Army days is once again borne out—don't volunteer.

Seriously, I want to thank Norm Pederson for allowing me to participate in this most important of days. I also want to thank him for his son, an intern in my office, who is the best third baseman in the Capitol Hill Softball League.

Far from being bored with the graduation season, I find occasions such as this remind me of what it is the power of a

---

[1] Delivered at the commencement exercises of the Brunswick School, Greenwich, Connecticut at 3 P.M., June 15, 1979. Quoted by permission.
[2] For biographical note, see Appendix.

United States Senator is supposed to be all about. It isn't to keep the world in place for the benefit of myself and other parents. Rather it is to try and make it a better place for you.

Anytime political survival even starts to look good I go to a graduation, to a playground, to a sheltered workshop invariably leaving these gathering places of the young renewed in the determination to do on behalf of the future those things no one else will touch with a ten foot pole. My job should always represent hope rather than safety. It's no different for your country. America must always be hope rather than geography. There can be no more permanence for a United States Senator than there is for the United States. In that sense I don't care about the position, I care very much about the job.

This approach has resulted in being called maverick, kook, flake or loner. Mark Russell once started his patter before the Connecticut Chamber of Commerce in Washington with the following introduction. "Republicans, Democrats, Independents, and Senator Weicker."

Today's speech then is not a defense of flakes and loners but an advocacy of them.

For example. The other day during the Greenwich Memorial Day Parade I saw one. An elderly man—white—marching with his black brothers and sisters in honor of *Brown vs The Board of Education*—the landmark civil rights decision of our generation.

The sight of him brought back memories. Specifically how at one time Alfred Baker Lewis was viewed as an oddball—even a Communist. Such was the background of today's hero. He fought with courage for equality under the Constitution for all our peoples—he fought alone—and he fought in Greenwich. If the life of Alfred Baker Lewis defines the words "oddball" and "Communist" may you all be one.

I think back to my days as First Selectman and the name Leslie Hand. "Right wing nut" thundered his opponents in the RTM [Representative Town Meeting]. "He's forever delaying progress." Yes, his was a different style. As I came to love this man I learned he was uncompromising in what he wished for as the quality of his town's endeavors. This commitment to excellence always consistent even when second best for reasons of time or money was the first choice of too many. If Leslie Hand made a few people think or a few more carry the day with facts and logic rather than casual emotion then "right wing nut" becomes an honor to which all of us should aspire.

Elsie Hill of Norwalk, Connecticut. It's ten years since her death and I have no doubt the question around the state would be the same as the one you're asking yourselves right now—who the hell is Elsie Hill?

From 1962, long before ERA was an honorable cause or even a cause to the day before she died not a month went by without me and every other officeholder receiving a call from Elsie Hill advocating women's rights. Eventually, most of us had our wives or secretaries listen to the rantings of this "lunatic" once we were told it was Miss Hill on the phone.

She died one week before the United States House of Representatives passed the ERA in 1970.

In preparation for today, I pulled out my floor speech of August 11, 1970.

I am proud to vote for this Constitutional guarantee of equal rights for women. But of even greater importance this is my way of officially recognizing the concept that one individual can have a profound effect on the policies and laws of our great United States.

Elsie Hill, what magnificent lunacy.

I recall the few moments of announcing what was to be my few days presidential campaign.

A "crazy" by the name of Ned Coll interrupted the proceedings to plead for equal job opportunities for minorities among Connecticut's congressional delegation.

This was the same "wild eyed SOB" who had stormed my offices in Washington and your beaches in Fairfield County . . . always on behalf of Connecticut's poor. I truly hope Ned Coll never becomes too old to become too outrageous. And I realize in saying that I'm pulling an unknown incident on some uncertain date down over my own head.

But in truth, ladies and gentlemen, the prick is to our conscience, it is not Ned Coll.

The date, August 28, 1968. Abraham Ribicoff, United States Senator from Connecticut, stands at the rostrum of the Democratic National Convention being held in Chicago, Illinois. Outside, America in the person of the local constabulary shows its darkest side in defense of the illogic of Vietnam.

The Senator chooses without hesitation between political courtesy and a nation's moral values and says for all of us what the Mayor of Chicago doesn't want to hear. When Richard Daley's middle finger goes into the air, Abraham Ribicoff is re-elected in Connecticut. Not because he accepted the insane world around him but because he defied it.

On May 4, 1970 the Ohio National Guard looked into the face of youth and pulled the trigger. Yes, I saw the films that showed unidentifiable forms scurrying to and fro—other forms motionless.

But it wasn't until I met Arthur Krause of Pittsburg, Pennsylvania that Kent State became wrong—very wrong.

After all, the Governor of Ohio said everything was all right—ditto the Commander of the Ohio National Guard. The President of the United States and the Attorney General said not to worry—that what had been done was proper. So who in their right mind could disagree.

Arthur Krause, Allison's father did. He spent ten years rectifying a terrible wrong—the death of his daughter and three other students. "But what do you expect from a grief crazed father the authorities asked?" "Humor him and eventually he'll go away." He didn't. And eventually it was the United States Government, not Arthur Krause, that came to its senses.

Allison was right—not her government. Art Krause was sane, not his government.

The list goes on. A black minister indicting a nation's lack of conscience from a jail cell in Montgomery, Alabama, and for his trials being smeared with charges of improper sexual activity and Communist affiliation by the law enforcement agencies of his (our country).

A young man from Connecticut sparking the turnabout of the once apathetic and put upon consumer being characterized by his detractors as acting out of financial self interest.

Let me stop here and say simply that this is a better world, a much better world because of Alfred Baker Lewis, Leslie Hand, Elsie Hill, Ned Coll, Abe Ribicoff, Dr. Martin Luther King, Ralph Nader and Art Krause.

Friends, young and old, I am told that these are times better devoted to nostalgia, to conformity, to retreat; to self.

I'm not advocating mass protests or a revolution. Those happenings involve thousands thus enjoying a popularity which immediately draws into question the propriety of the cause.

No. Be a flake, a loner, a kook, a maverick on behalf of somebody or something.

These are great concepts of the Bill of Rights that need advocacy.

There are people out there more than you can imagine who are hurt, who are poor, who are starving, who are without hope—and who have been very much left alone. So bring one home—not to your parent's house but to your heart.

To do that and especially to do it alone will make you the envy of the world.

RISK AND OTHER FOUR-LETTER WORDS[1]

WALTER B. WRISTON[2]

Have Americans placed their material well-being above the challenge of growth and conquering new frontiers? Is the uncertainty of these seventies the cause of their hesitancy at risktaking? Is society seeking "an impossible physical and economic security?"

[1] Delivered at a banquet of the Economic Club of Chicago, meeting in the Grand Ballroom of the Palmer House, Chicago, Il. at 6 P.M. October 25, 1979. Quoted by permission.
[2] For biographical note, see Appendix.

Walter B. Wriston, chairman of Citicorp, observes that "The driving force of our society is the conviction that risktaking and individual responsibilities are the ways to advance our mutual fortunes."

Mr. Wriston's remarks were made at a 6 P.M., black tie dinner of the Economic Club of Chicago in the Grand Ballroom of the Palmer House on October 25, 1979. The audience, one of the largest in the Club's history (founded in 1927), was composed of 655 club members and 741 guests.

The Wriston speech echoes the mounting revolt against government—bureaucracy, high taxation, and excessive regulation. Tax revolts are gaining momentum in many states; politicians are moved toward deregulation of aviation, trucking, and petroleum production; some want to return many functions to the states; others question whether benefits of environmental protection outweigh the costs. Wriston sums up an increasingly popular sentiment that our safe, risk-free (and also stagnant) society, dominated by protective government is stifling adventuresome spirit and brave initiative. The audience—from the business and professional community—enthusiastically agreed with his statement: "Be nice, feel guilty, and play safe. If there was ever a prescription for producing a dismal future, that has to be it. It is a sure prescription for the demise of our way of life."

The men and women who founded our country were at once adventurers who took personal risks of the most extreme kind and pragmatists who wrote a Constitution based on the tested theory that men are not gods. No assumptions were made that elected leaders would all be selfless persons devoted to the public interest. Rather, the rock upon which our structure rests is a Constitution that diffuses power, lest one person or group grow too powerful. Alexander Hamilton put it succinctly when he said, "If men were angels no government would be necessary." The system they devised based on this assumption about human nature has stood the test of time. Our government has proved to be one of the most enduring in history.

While the constitutional framework set limits on power, the driving force of our society is the conviction that risktaking and individual responsibility are the ways to advance our mutual fortunes. Our founding Fathers were themselves political adventurers and fighters who did not hesitate to sign a document pledging "our Lives, our Fortunes, and our sacred Honor" in pursuit of a brighter future against overwhelming odds. They would have been more than a little surprised to learn that what they were really fighting for was a totally predictable, risk-free society.

Today, however, the idea is abroad in the land that the descendants of these bold adventurers should all be sheltered from risk and uncertainty as part of our natural heritage. We seem to have raised a generation of advocates, writers, and bureaucrats to whom the word "risk" is an acceptable term only when used in connection with promoting a state lottery. Emerson's counsel, "Always do what you are afraid to do," is now rejected as too upsetting, and one should steer the safe noncontroversial course. One has only to look at the gray stagnation of planned societies where this idea is far advanced to wonder how such a system can continue to attract so much intellectual support. But it does.

It can be argued that if the desire to avoid risk above all else becomes the predominant objective of American society, it may in the end destroy not only our economic system but our form of government along with it. At bottom, democracy itself rests on an act of faith, on a belief in individual responsibility and the superiority of the free marketplace, both intellectual and economic, over anything that might be devised for us by a committee of bureaucrats disguised as guardian angels. There is real reason to fear that those who do not share that faith, in their efforts to build a risk-free society, have in fact not only drained the spirit of our people but have already seriously impaired the viability of the most productive economic system that the world has ever seen.

This is a relatively new problem for Americans. The whole of this country was opened up by people who were— no less than the Founding Fathers—at once adventurers and patriots. My own grandmother, in company with hundreds more, went west in a Conestoga wagon, which by today's standards was unsafe at any speed. The environmental problems were enormous. They used buffalo dung to fuel their campfires. Half of the wagon train in which my grandmother traveled was massacred by Indians. But many more followed in their tracks along trails which today no government agency at a city, state, or federal level would think of certifying as safe for travelers. In fact, the pioneers would probably not even be allowed to settle down at the end of their journey. The sparkling, exciting city of San Francisco was built and rebuilt on a set of hills that would test the footing of a mountain goat. And if that is not bad enough, it lies along the San Andreas earthquake fault which has already destroyed it once. No modern urban planner could possibly approve the building of San Francisco today. The risk would be said to be too great.

The unremitting atmosphere of protective custody which now seems to surround us is producing a new kind of national mood. The American spirit of optimism and enterprise is being overwhelmed by a malaise perhaps best described by the English journalist, Henry Fairlie, when he wrote:

If the American people for the first time no longer believe that life will be better for their children, it is at least in part because they are beginning to think that there will be no food which their children will be able to eat without dying like rats of cancer, no form of transport that will be considered safe enough to get them from here to there, and in fact nothing that their children may safely do except sit like Narcissus by a riverbank and gaze at their wan and delicate forms as they throw the last speck of Granola to the fish.

This is a far cry from the spirit of enterprise that turned a raw continent into a great nation. Of course, there have always been those among us who bewail all forms of risk: political, economic, or personal. They are the ones who have never understood the Biblical injunction, "For whosoever will save his life shall lose it." But such people of little faith did not always have a nationwide, instant forum for their timid views nor the power to enforce them upon others. When the great English constitutional scholar, Lord Bryce, uttered his judgment that the American "Constitution is all sail and no anchor," his verdict was not proclaimed electronically around the world. In fact, it passed almost unnoticed. There was no clamor for a new constitutional convention to remedy our disastrous mistake, so clearly identified by an "expert." Today, however, we all live in Marshall McLuhan's "global village," and Chicken Little runs through the square twice a day.

In times past, ideas spread by pamphleteers and later on in books and by the press. Great centers of learning grew up which refined and nurtured ideas and passed them on from one generation to another. This same function was also performed by the churches. Today, a pop phrase rooted in some private discontent, some transient desire to transfer responsibility for one's own actions to somebody else, or some simpleminded panacea for complex problems, is echoed and re-echoed throughout the land in a matter of minutes on the 7 o'clock news.

The signs carried by a hundred protestors on the site of a nuclear plant may be seen instantly by 50 million Americans in living color. Contrast the impact of this with the great draft riots in New York in 1863 where mobs ranged over the city for four days and four nights, looting and burning. It was only on the fifth day that 6,000 federal troops poured into the city and order was restored. Most Americans living at that time never heard of the incident. One of the so-called "volunteer special" policemen who was involved in the riot said, "No adequate account of the draft riot of 1863 has ever been printed."

Today cameras zoom in on the face of the man struck by the rock or the policeman's club. I do not argue here that this is bad, far from it. But I have to observe that, for the first time in the history of man, our life with all the flaws inherent in human nature, all the breakdowns in technology, and all of our social foibles is communicated instantly to the world. Things will inevitably go wrong, because men still are not gods. But because all the failures, the mistakes, and the accidents intrude upon our consciousness in an almost unbroken stream, the clamor grows for a fail-safe society.

This growing thirst for an impossible physical and economic security has a direct bearing on whether or not we will maintain our spiritual and political freedom. The relevance of risk to liberty is direct and clear. For in the end, it always turns out that the only way to avoid risk is to leap into the arms of an all-knowing government. George Gilder [writer] put it best when he wrote:

Strangely enough, the man who sees a future blighted by coercion and scarcity also tends to believe that the present can be made as free of risk and uncertainty as the past, receding reassuringly in the reliable lenses of hindsight. He calls upon government to create an orderly and predictable economy with known energy reserves always equaling prospective needs; with jobs always assured in current geographic and demographic patterns; with monetary demand always expanding to absorb expected output of current corporate goods; with disorderly foreign intruders banished from the marketplace or burdened by tariffs and quotas; with invention and creativity summoned by the bureaucrats for forced marches of research and development; with inflation insurance in every contract and unemployment insurance in every job; with all windfall wealth briskly taxed away and unseemly poverty removed by income guarantees. In this view, risk and uncertainty are seen to be the problem and government the solution in the fail-safe quest for a managed economy of steady and predictable long-term growth.

If you carry this logic to its bitter end, it all gets reduced to the motto under the picture of Mussolini which plastered Italy at the height of his power. It said, "He Will Decide." The responsibility no longer belonged to the individual. The leader would decide. The pattern is always the same. A bureaucracy is put in place to coerce the people into doing something for "their own good." The bureaucracy then assumes a life of its own, and the coercion continues as the bureaucracy's primary task, long after the original purpose has been forgotten. The Securities and Exchange Commission was created in response to a felt need to protect the investor against fraud. It was a worthy objective, but little by little its role has expanded until now it's attempting to dictate everything from how a board of directors should govern a company to how lawyers should exercise their professional judgment. The ultimate in what now seems to be the trend in corporate governance, incidentally, was achieved by the City Bank as long ago as 1844, when we had nine employees, but fifteen directors who assisted in the day-to-day operations. If we are obliged to revive that ratio, we are going to end up with 83,-000 new directors.

Our American economic system, like our political system, is untidy—it offends those people who love tidy, predictable societies. We make a lot of mistakes in this country, we have a lot of failures. Some people see only the failures; they cannot seem to grasp the fact that the failures are the price we pay for the successes. It's as though they wanted to have "up" without "down" or "hot" without "cold."

We read in our newspapers, and even in our business magazines, solemn words about "risky investments" and "risky loans" from writers who do not seem to realize that these phrases are as redundant as talking about a one-story bungalow. All investments and all loans are risky because they are all based on educated guesses about the future rather than the certain knowledge of what will happen. Despite the most sophisticated market research, no one really knows if the public will buy the product or use the service which we are about to produce. The new product might be an Edsel with a $400 million price tag, or it might be Peter Goldmark's long-playing record. It could be the decision of a Joe Wilson, risking all the resources of his small company to make a copier later called Xerox, and doing it in the face of a careful study which showed that it would be a bad substitute for the familiar carbon paper.

The odds against success of any kind in our society are formidable. Some 300,000 businesses are started each year in America, and only about a third of them survive as long as five years. Proponents of a safe, stagnant, boring tomorrow view this as a wasteful process, to say nothing of its being irrational. On the contrary. George Gilder has argued:

. . . such waste and irrationality is the secret of economic growth. Because no one knows which venture will succeed . . . a society ruled by faith and risk rather than by rational calculus, a society open to the future rather than planning it, will call forth an endless stream of innovation, enterprise, and art.

Our bookshelves today are piled high with books warning us that the pace of change has become too much for human beings to tolerate, that it is not just risk that people fear, but the future itself. We are being overwhelmed, we're told, by new technology. When we see what the electronic computer has done and is doing to the world, and consider that it was invented in 1946, this argument may seem plausible. But go back a hundred years to 1846 and the argument falls apart.

That was the year Brigham Young led the Mormons out of Illinois on the way to Utah—and coincidentally the year that saw the invention of the sewing machine and the steel moldboard plow. Historians have called the period that began then and lasted to the outbreak of World War I the "heroic age" of invention. From the sewing machine in 1846 to the radio vacuum tube in 1911, a major new invention appeared on the average of every 15 to 18 months, and was followed almost immediately by a new industry based on the invention. That's what the last half of the nineteenth century was like, but there were few voices then calling, "Stop the world, I want to get off."

There were a few, of course. Not long after Lee De Forest invented the vacuum tube amplifier, he was arrested for stock fraud. He'd been going around saying that his service would be able to transmit the human voice across the Atlantic. At his trial, the prosecuting attorney said: "Based on his absurd and deliberately misleading statement, the public, your Honor, has been persuaded to purchase stock in his company."

The jury acquitted De Forest, but the judge admonished him to forget his crackpot inventions and go "get a common, garden-type job and stick to it."

If De Forest were inventing his gadget today, and he could convince people it worked, he might still be in trouble. Before he could go into production, there would probably be a long delay while committees were formed to study the environmental impact of bouncing radio waves off the ionosphere.

The people who insist on seeing only the failures have still another debilitating effect on our society: they frequently manage to make us feel guilty even about our successes.

Malaria, for thousands of years the number-one killer of human beings, was finally brought under control after World War II by DDT. But instead of hearing about the tens of millions of human lives that have been saved over the past 30 years, we are told about the damage to our natural environment. Concern for the environment is obviously justified, but the highly publicized demonstrations, complete with rock stars and movie actresses, would have us believe that man, and particularly his technology, is single-handedly polluting what would otherwise be a pure and benign Nature, something like Disneyland on a nice day in September. Michael Novak recently reminded us that this just is not so. He wrote:

Nature was raw and cruel to nature long before human beings intervened. It may be doubted whether human beings have ever done one-tenth of the polluting to nature that nature has done to itself. There is infinitely more methane gas—poisonous in one respect, and damaging to the environment—generated by the swamps of Florida and other parts of the United States than by all the automobile pollution of all the places on this planet. In our superhuman efforts to be nice and feel guilty, we sometimes try to take all the credit for pollution improperly.

Be nice, feel guilty, and play safe. If there was ever a prescription for producing a dismal future, that has to be it. It is a sure prescription for the demise of our way of life.

It is almost impossible to exaggerate the importance to the general welfare of the willingness of individuals to take a personal risk. The worst thing that can happen to a society, as to an individual, is to become terrified of uncertainty. Uncertainty is an invitation to innovate, to create; uncertainty is the blank page in the author's typewriter, the granite block before a sculptor, the capital in the hands of an investor, or the problem challenging the inventive mind of a scientist or an engineer. In short, uncertainty is the opportunity to make the world a better place. Despite this, everything in our national life today seems designed to encourage our natural caution, urging us to play it safe, to invent a risk-free system and give up being tough-minded. The tax structure discourages the innovators, penalizes the successful, and preserves the inefficient. Even many medicines in common use around the world to prevent human suffering are denied to Americans on the slender grounds that an overdosed mouse has contracted a tumor. This is not prudence. Prudence is one of the intellectual virtues, and there is very little intelligence to be found in all this. It is institutionalized timidity, and I submit that it does not represent the will of the vast majority of the American people.

If we observe the world around us Americans as individuals seek out risk. Every child who plays football, or hockey, or any other contact sport, risks injury. There is no shortage of test pilots for new aircraft, nor candidates for any of the other hazardous jobs in our society, including the job of President of the United States. If we perceive that life is too easy, we put sand traps and other obstacles on the golf course and create artificial hazards where none exist. In short, risk is a necessary part of life and one which belongs on our list of natural rights.

Let those who seek a perpetual safe harbor continue to do so. Let them renounce risk for themselves, if they choose. What no one has a right to do is renounce it for all the rest of us, or to pursue the chimerical goal of a risk-free society for some by eliminating the rewards of risk for everyone.

The society which promises no risks and whose leaders use the word "risk" only as a pejorative may be able to protect life, but there will be no liberty, and very little pursuit of happiness. You will look in vain in the Federalist Papers, the Declaration of Independence, or the Constitution for promises of a safe, easy, risk-free life. Indeed, when Woodrow Wilson called for "a world safe for democracy," it was left to Gilbert Chesterton to put that sentiment in perspective. "Impossible," he said, "democracy is a dangerous trade."

APPENDIX

BIOGRAPHICAL NOTES

BRADEN, WALDO WARDER (1911–   ). Born, Blakensburg, Iowa; B.A., Penn College, 1932; M.A., University of Iowa, 1938, Ph.D., 1942; teacher, Fremont (Iowa) High School, 1933–35; Mt. Pleasant (Iowa) High School, 1935–38; instructor and dean of students, Iowa Wesleyan College, 1938–40, 1942–43, 1946; AUS, 1943–45; associate professor, Louisiana State University, 1946–51, professor, 1951–73; Boyd professor, 1973–79; emeritus, 1979–   ; chairman of Department of Speech, 1958–1976; executive secretary, Speech Communication Association, 1954–57, president, 1961–62; president, Southern Speech Communication Association, 1969–70; distinguished service award of Speech Communication Association, 1978; author: *Public Speaking, Principles and Practice* (with Gray) (1951, 1963); *Oran Decision-Making* (with Brandenburg) (1955); *Speech Practices* (with Gehring) (1958); *Public Speaking: The Essentials* (1966); *Broadcasting and the Public Interest* (with Pennybacker) (1969); *Speech Criticism* (with Thonssen and Baird) (1970); *Speech Methods and Resources* (with others) (1961, 1972); editor: *Oratory in the Old South* (1970); *Oratory in the New South* (1979); *The Speech Teacher,* 1967–69; *Representative American Speeches,* ten annual volumes (1970–1980); contributor to numerous other volumes and author of numerous articles in speech and history journals.

BRAY, CHARLES W. III (1933–   ). Born New York City; B.A., magna cum laude, Princeton University, 1955; Fulbright Fellow, University of Bordeaux, 1956; graduate study, University of Maryland; foreign service officer, US State Department 1958–67, serving in the Philippines and Central African Republic; special assistant to Deputy Under Secretary for Political Affairs and other offices, 1967–1971; director of Office of Press Relations, Department of State; 1971–1975 deputy assistant secretary for Public Affairs, 1974–76; deputy assistant secretary for Inter-American Affairs, 1976–77; deputy director, International Communication Agency, 1977–

BRENNAN, WILLIAM JOSEPH, JR. (1906–   ). Born, Newark, New Jersey; B.S., University of Pennsylvania, Wharton School of

Business, 1928; LL.B., Harvard University, 1931; honorary degrees, Suffolk University, 1956; New York University, 1957; Colgate University, 1957; Rutgers, 1958; Jewish Theological Seminary, 1964; George Washington University, 1965; Notre Dame University, 1968; Harvard University, 1968; admitted to New Jersey bar, 1931; practiced law in Newark, 1932–42; 1945–49; trial judge, New Jersey Superior Court, 1949–50; Appellate Division, 1950–52; associate justice of New Jersey Supreme Court, 1952–56; associate justice, US Supreme Court, 1956–   ; colonel, US Army, 1942–45, Legion of Merit. (See also *Current Biography: June* 1957.)

CARTER, JIMMY (JAMES EARL CARTER JR.) (1924–   ). Born, Plains, Georgia; student, Georgia Southwestern University, 1941–42; Georgia Institute of Technology, 1942–43; B.S., US Naval Academy, 1946; postgraduate instruction, nuclear physics, Union College, 1952; honorary degrees: Morris Brown College, Morehouse College, Notre Dame University and Georgia Institute of Technology; US Navy, 1947–53, advancing through grades to lieutenant commander; resigned 1953; farmer, warehouseman, 1953–77; served two terms in Georgia senate (Democrat), 1962–66 (voted most effective member); governor, 1971–74; chairman, Democratic National Campaign Committee, 1974; US President, 1977–   ; past president, Georgia Planning Association; first chairman, West Central Georgia Planning and Development Commission; author; *Why Not the Best* (1975). (See also *Current Biography: November* 1977.)

COX, ARCHIBALD (1912–   ). Born, Plainfield, New Jersey; B.A., Harvard, 1934; LL.B., magna cum laude, 1937; honorary degrees: Loyola University, 1964; University of Chicago, 1964; University of Cincinnati, 1967; University of Denver, 1974; Amherst College, 1974; Rutgers University, 1974; University of Michigan, 1976; Wheaton College, 1977; admitted, Massachusetts bar, 1937; private law practice, Ropes, Gray, Best, Coolidge, & Rugg, Boston, 1938–41; attorney, solicitor general's office, US Department of Justice, 1941–43; associate solicitor, US Department of Labor, 1943–45; lecturer, Harvard Law School, 1945–46; professor of law, 1946–61; Williston professor of law, 1965–76; Carl M. Loeb University professor 1976–   ; solicitor general, US Department of Justice, 1966; special Watergate prosecutor, 1973; author: *Law and the National Labor Policy* (1960), *Civil Rights, the Constitution and the Courts* (with Mark DeWolfe Howe and J. R. Wiggins)

(1967), *The Warren Court* (1968), *Cases on Labor Law* (with Derek C. Bok) (1969), *Role of the Supreme Court in American Government* (1976). (See also *Current Biography: July* 1961.)

HATFIELD, MARK ODOM (1922–   ). Born, Dallas, Oregon; B.A., Willamette University, 1943; M.A., Stanford University, 1948; numerous honorary degrees; resident assistant, Stanford University, 1947–49; instructor, political science, Willamette University, 1949; dean of students, associate professor, 1950–56; member, Oregon House of Representatives, 1951–55; member, Oregon Senate, 1955–57; secretary of state, Oregon, 1957–59; governor, 1959–67; member, US Senate (Republican, Oregon), 1967–   ; USNR, 1943–46; author: *Not Quite So Simple* (1967), *Conflict and Conscience* (1971), *Between a Rock and a Hard Place* (1976). (See also *Current Biography: November* 1959.)

HESBURGH, THEODORE MARTIN (1917–   ). Born, Syracuse, New York; student, University of Notre Dame, 1934–37; Ph.B., Gregorian University, Rome, Italy, 1939; S.T.L., Holy Cross College, 1943; S.T.D., Catholic University of America, 1945; honorary degrees from seventy-two institutions; entered Order of the Congregation of Holy Cross, 1943; ordained to priesthood, 1943; assistant professor of religion, University of Notre Dame, and head of department of religion, 1948–49; executive vice president, University of Notre Dame, 1949–52; president 1952–   ; fellow, American Academy of Arts and Sciences; Medal of Freedom, 1964; member, United States Commission on Civil Rights; chairman, 1969; member, Carnegie Commission on the Future of Higher Education; Board of Trustees, Rockefeller Foundation; United Negro College Fund, Inc.; Eleanor Roosevelt Memorial Foundation; and Carnegie Foundation for the Advancement of Teaching; board of directors, American Council on Education; Freedoms Foundation at Valley Forge; Education Development Center; member, President's General Advisory Committee on Foreign Assistance Programs; President's Commission on an All-Volunteer Armed Force; also numereous other boards and committees; author of many books, including *God and the World of Man* (1950), *Patterns for Educational Growth* (1958), *Thoughts for Our Times* (1962), *More Thoughts for Our Times* (1965), *Still More Thoughts for Our Times* (1966), *Thoughts IV,* (1968), *Thoughts V* (1969), *The Human Imperative* (1974), *The Hesburgh Papers* (1979); recipient of forty special awards and honors. (See also *Current Biography: January* 1955.)

HIATT, HOWARD H. (1925–   ). Born, Patchhogue, New York; M.D., Harvard University, 1948; Beth Israel Hospital, Boston, 1948–50; research fellow, Cornell Medical College, 1950–53; clinical investigator, USPHS, 1953–55; faculty, Harvard Medical School, 1955–   ; H. L. Blumgart professor of medicine, 1963–72; professor 1972–   ; physician-in-chief, Beth Israel Hospital, 1963–72; dean, Harvard School of Public Health, 1972–

HOLTZMAN, ELIZABETH (1941–   ). Born, Brooklyn, New York; B.A., magna cum laude, Radcliffe College, 1962; J.D., Harvard University, 1965; honorary degree, Regis College, 1976; admitted to New York Bar 1966, practiced law in New York City, 1965–72; assistant to mayor, New York City, 1967–70; member, US House of Representatives (Democrat, New York), 1973–   ; founder and co-chairman of Congresswoman's Caucus; Phi Beta Kappa; recipient numerous awards. (See also *Current Biography: November* 1973.)

HOWE, HAROLD II (1918–   ). Born, Hartford, Connecticut; A.B., Yale University, 1940; M.A., Columbia University, 1947; additional work, University of Cincinnati, 1953–57; Harvard University, 1960; honorary degrees: Princeton University; St. Louis University; Notre Dame University; Shaw University; Adelphi College; USNR, 1941–45; teacher, Darrow School, New Lebanon, New York, 1940–41; Phillips Academy, Andover, Massachusetts, 1947–50; principal, Andover junior high school, 1950–53; Walnut Hills high school, Cincinnati, 1953–57; Newton (Massachusetts) high school, 1957–60; superintendent of schools, Scarsdale, New York, 1960–64; director, North Carolina Learning Institute, 1964–65; US Commissioner of Education, 1965–68; vice president, Division of Education and Research, Ford Foundation, 1969–   ; trustee, College Entrance Examination Board; Yale University; member, Commission on the Humanities. (See also *Current Biography: November* 1967.)

JORDAN, VERNON E. JR. (1935–   ). Born, Atlanta, Georgia; B.A., DePauw University, 1957; first prize, Indiana Interstate Oratorical Contest, sophomore year; J.D., Howard University, 1960; honorary degrees from fifteen institutions; circuit vice president of American Law Students Association while at Howard University; helped to desegregate the University of Georgia; clerk in law office of civil rights attorney Donald Hollowell; field secretary, NAACP, Georgia branch, 1962; set up law partnership in Arkansas with another civil rights lawyer, Wiley A. Barnton, 1964; director,

Voter Education Project for the Southern Regional Council, 1964–68; executive director, United Negro College Fund, 1970–72; director, National Urban League, January 1972– ; member, Arkansas and Georgia bar associations; US Supreme Court bar; American Bar Association; Common Cause; Rockefeller Foundation; Twentieth Century Fund; other service organizations; has held fellowships at Harvard University's Institute of Politics, the John F. Kennedy School of Government, and the Metropolitan Applied Research Center; serves on boards of several corporations. (See also *Current Biography: February* 1972.)

KISSINGER, HENRY ALFRED (1923–). Born, Fuerth, Germany; B.A., summa cum laude, Harvard, 1950; M.A., 1952; Ph.D., 1954; arrived United States, 1938; naturalized, 1943; executive director Harvard International Seminar, 1951–60; lecturer, government, Harvard University, 1957–59; associate professor, 1959–62; professor, 1962–69; consultant to Presidents Eisenhower, Kennedy, Johnson; assistant to President Nixon for national security affairs, 1969–74; director, NSC, 1969–75; secretary, US Department of State, 1973–77; faculty, Georgetown University, 1977– ; consultant, NBC, 1977– ; AUS, 1943–46; Nobel peace prize, 1973; author: *Nuclear Weapons and Foreign Policy* (1957), *A World Restored* (1957), *The Necessity For Choice: Prospects of American Foreign Policy* (1961), *The Troubled Partnership: A Reappraisal of the Atlantic Alliance* (1965), *American Foreign Policy: Three Essays* (1969), *White House Years* (1979); over forty articles in professional journals. (See also *Current Biography: June* 1972.)

LUCE, CLARE BOOTH (1903–). Born, New York City, New York; educated at St. Mary's, Garden City, New York, 1915–17; and the Castle, Tarrytown, New York, 1917–19; honorary degrees: Colby College, Fordham University, Mundelein College, Temple University, Creighton University; Georgetown University, Seton Hall College, Mt. Holyoke College, Boston University; associate editor, *Vogue Magazine*, 1930; associate editor *Vanity Fair Magazine;* managing editor, 1933–34; newspaper columnist, 1934; playwright, 1935; US House of Representatives, 1943–47. US Ambassador to Italy, 1953–57; author: *Stuffed Shirts* (1933), *Europe in the Spring* (1940), (ed.) *Saints for Now* (1952), *Abide With Me* (1937), *The Women* (1937), *Kiss the Boys Goodbye* (1938), *Margin for Error* (1939), *Come to the Stable* (1947), *Child of the Morning* (1951), *Slam the Door Softly* (1970); numerous awards. (See also *Current Biography: April* 1953.)

MONDALE, WALTER FREDERICK (1928–   ). Born, Ceylon, Minnesota; B.A., cum laude, University of Minnesota, 1951; LL.B., 1956; admitted to Minnesota bar, 1956; private practice of law, 1956–60; attorney general, state of Minnesota, 1960–64; US Senate (Democrat, Minnesota), 1964–77; AUS, 1951–53; US Vice President, 1977–   ; member, National Security Council, 1977–   ; Regent, Smithsonian Institution, 1977–   ; author: *The Accountability of Power: Toward a Responsible Presidency* (1976). (See also *Current Biography: May* 1978.)

SCHMITT, HARRISON HAGAN (1935–   ). Born, Santa Rita, New Mexico; B.S., California Institute of Technology, 1957; Fulbright Fellowship, University of Oslo, 1957–58; Ph.D., in Geology, Harvard University, 1964; honorary degree, Colorado School of Mines, 1973; US Geological Survey, 1964–65; astronaut NASA, 1965–74; lunar module pilot and geologist, Apollo 17, 1972; landed on moon in the valley of Taurus-Littrow, 1972; assistant administrator NASA, 1974–75; US Senate (Republican, New Mexico), 1977–   ; Johnson Space Center Superior Achievement award, 1970; distinguished service medal NASA, 1973; Arthur S. Fleming Award, 1973. (See also *Current Biography: July* 1974.)

SEVAREID, (ARNOLD) ERIC (1912–   ). Born, Velva, North Dakota; B.A., University of Minnesota, 1935; attended the London School of Economics and the Alliance in Paris; reporter and editor of the Paris edition of the New York *Herald Tribune*, 1938–39; worked in France with Edward R. Murrow, Columbia Broadcasting System, 1939–41; CBS News Bureau, Washington, D.C., 1941–43; war correspondent, in Asia, 1943–44; in Europe, 1944–45; CBS Washington Bureau, 1946–59; roving European correspondent, CBS, 1959–61; moderator, CBS telecasts of Town Meeting of the World, The Great Challenge, Years of Crisis, and Where We Stand; CBS Evening News with Walter Cronkite from Washington, 1964–1977, consultant- ; author: *Canoeing With the Cree* (1935), *Not So Wild a Dream* (1946), *In One Ear* (1952), *Small Sounds in the Night* (1956), *This Is Eric Sevareid* (1964), *Candidates, 1960* (1959); received numerous awards; past president, Radio Correspondents. (See also *Current Biography: October* 1966.)

SPETH, GUS (JAMES GUSTAVE) (1942–   ). Born, Orangeburg, South Carolina; B.A., Yale University, 1964, LL.B., 1969. Rhodes scholar, Balliol College, Oxford University, 1966; Columbia, 1969; admitted to D.C. bar, 1969; law clerk to Hugo L. Black of US Supreme Court, 1969–70; staff attorney, National Resources Defense

Council, 1970–77; member, Council of Environmental Quality, 1977–

SULLIVAN, JOHN H. (1935–   ). Born, Toledo, Ohio; A.B.A., Marquette University, 1951; M.A., 1961; Ph.D., American University, 1969; instructor, Marquette University, 1957–59; reporter, Springfield (Ohio) *Sun* and Milwaukee *Sentinel*, 1959–62; staff assistant, US Representative Clement J. Zablocki (Democrat, Wisconsin), 1962–69; senior staff consultant, US House of Representatives Foreign Affairs Committee, 1961–77; special assistant to AID administrator, 1977; assistant administrator for Asia, Agency for International Development, 1977–

WEICKER, LOWELL P. JR. (1931–   ). Born, Paris, France; B.A., Yale University, 1953; LL.B., University of Virginia School of Law, 1958; admitted, Connecticut bar, 1960; private law practice, several years; member, Connecticut State Assembly, 1963–69; 1st selectman, Greenwich, 1964–68; member, US House of Representatives (Republican, Connecticut), 1969–71; member, US Senate, 1971–   ; US Army, 1953–55; US Army Reserve, 1959–64. (See also *Current Biography: January* 1974.)

WRISTON, WALTER BIGELOW (1919–   ). Born, Middletown, Connecticut; B.A. with distinction, Wesleyan University, 1941; M.A., Fletcher School International Law, Tufts University, 1942; honorary degrees: Lawrence College, 1962; Tufts University, 1963; Brown University, 1969; Columbia University, 1972; Pace University, 1974; St Johns University, 1974; Lafayette College, 1975; Fordham University, 1977; New York University, 1977; officer, special division, US Department of State, 1941–42; US Army, 1942–46; joined staff, Citibank, 1946; president, 1967–70; chairman and chief executive officer of Citicorp, 1970–   ; director of several corporations. (See also *Current Biography: November* 1977.)

WYDLER, JOHN W. (1924–   ). Born, Brooklyn, New York; attended Brown University, 1941–42; 1945–47; LL.B., Harvard University Law School, 1950; admitted to New York bar, 1950; private practice of law, 1950–53; US Attorney, Office for Eastern District of New York, 1953–59; private practice of law, 1959–   ; US House of Representatives (Republican, New York), 1963–   ; AUS, 1942–45; Phi Beta Kappa at Brown University.

CUMULATIVE AUTHOR INDEX

1970-1971–1979-1980

A cumulative author index to the volumes of REPRESENTA-TIVE AMERICAN SPEECHES for the years 1937–1938 through 1959–1960 appears in the 1959–1960 volume and for the years 1960–1961 through 1969–1970 in the 1969–1970 volume.